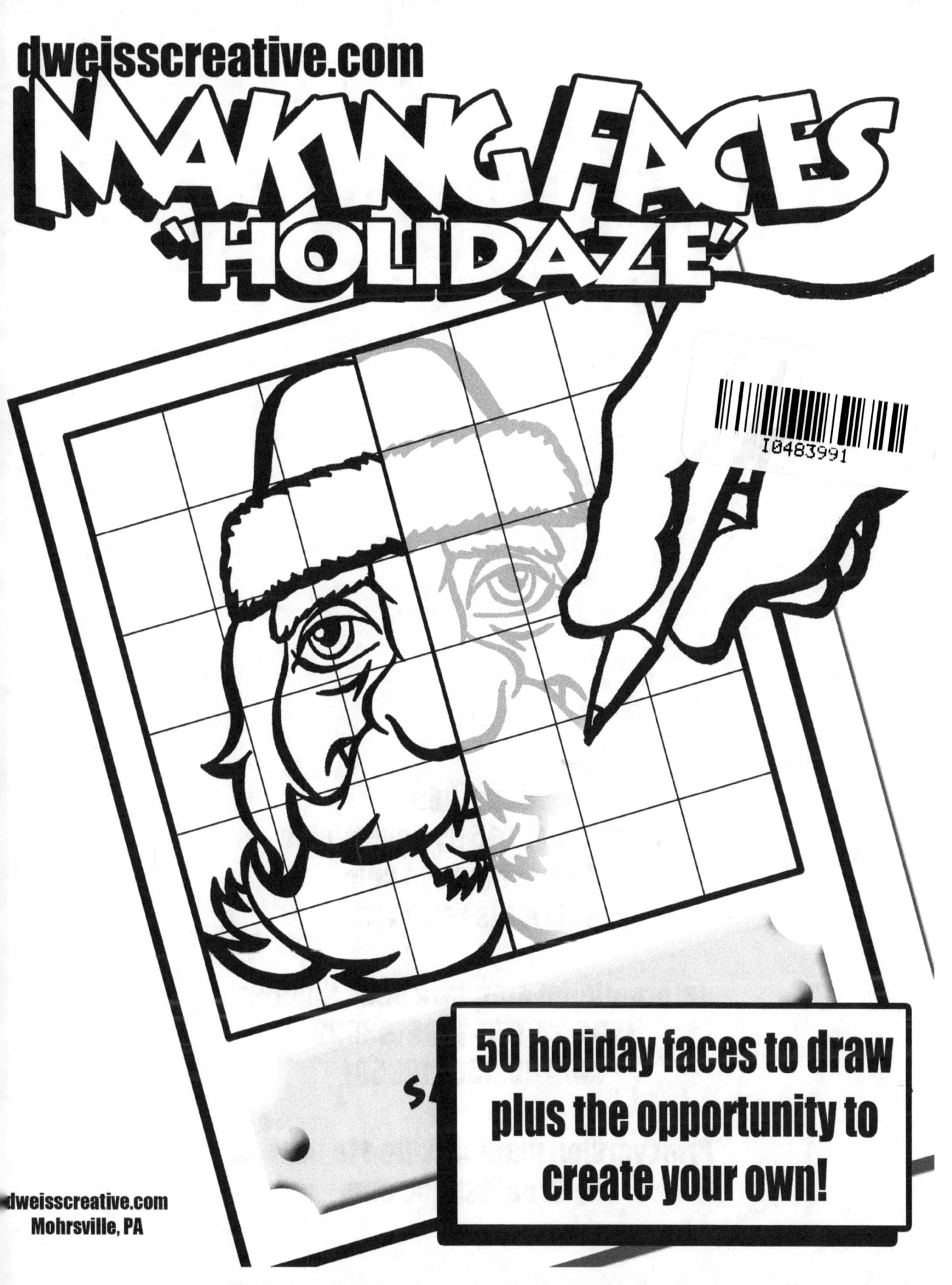

SO HOW DOES THIS WORK?

Let's start by drawing Santa...

1. Start in the center and duplicate what you see in the opposite square only backwards.

2. Work your way down the page and across the grid until the drawing is complete, copying as closely as you can.

3. When you finish, add color and decorate your picture.

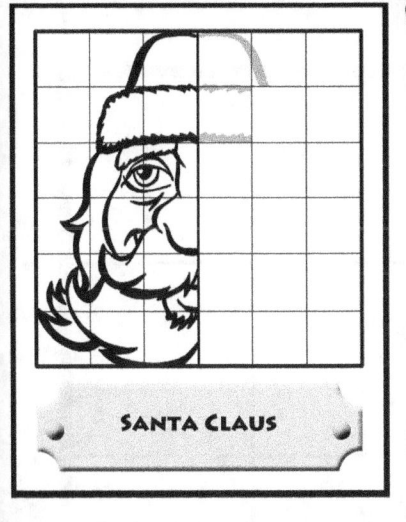

SANTA CLAUS

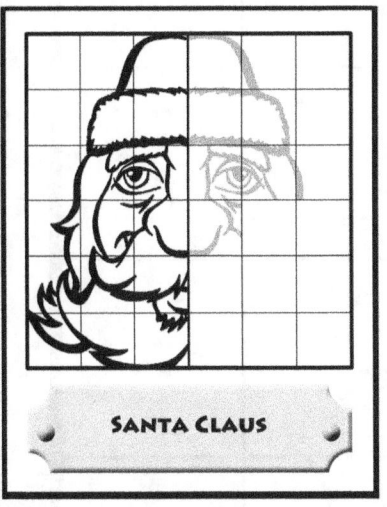

SANTA CLAUS

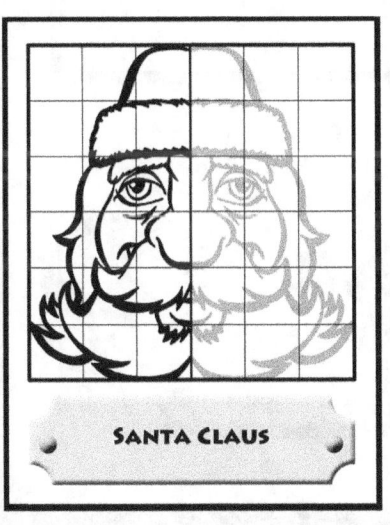

SANTA CLAUS

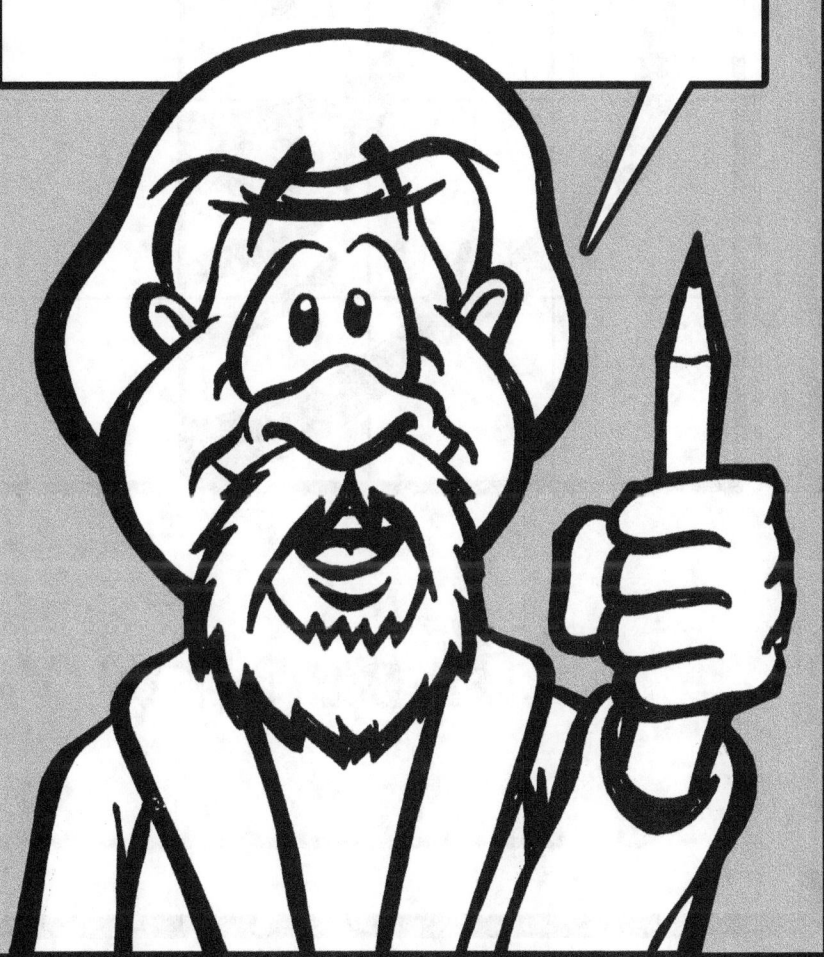

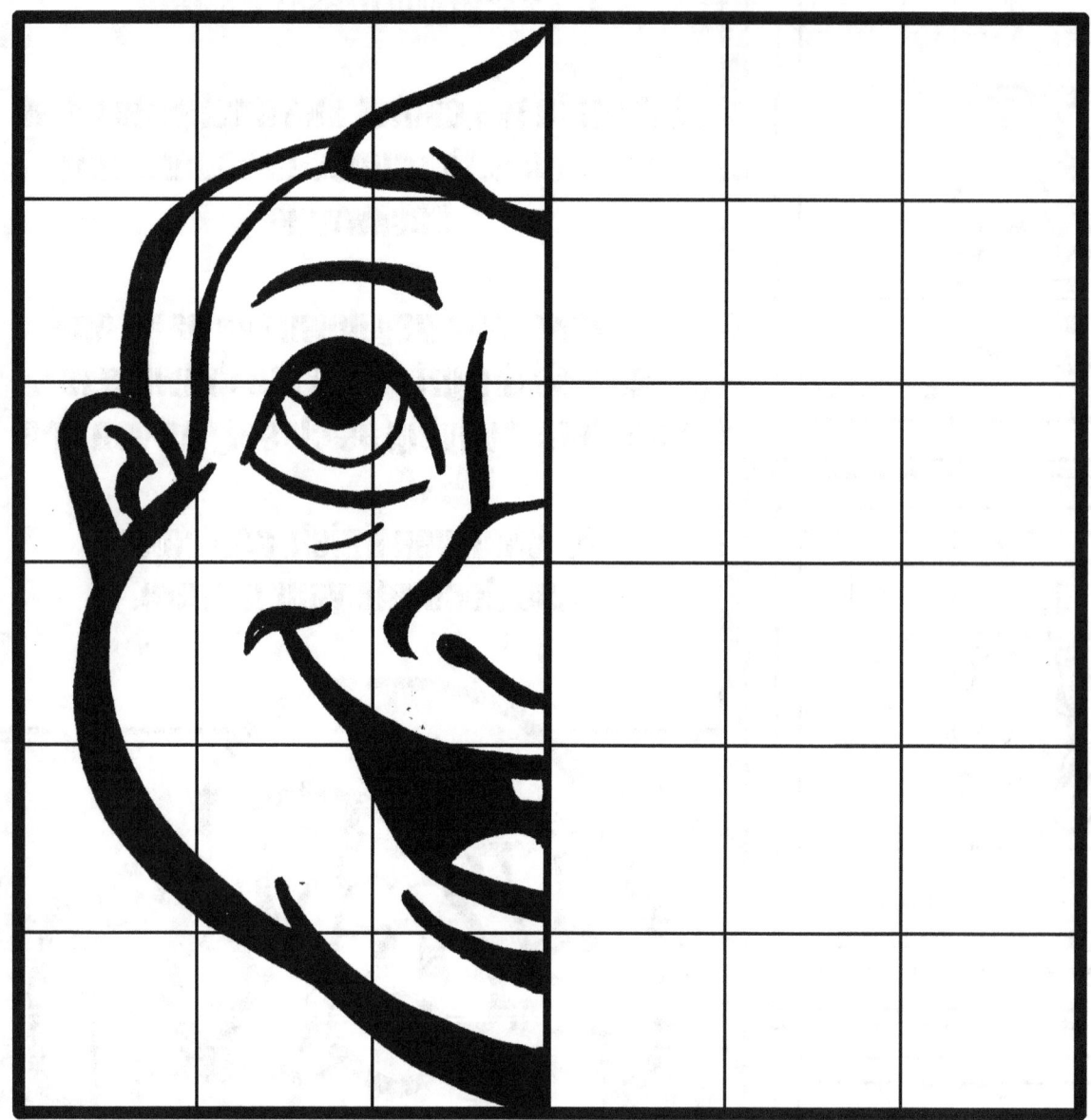

BABY NEW YEAR

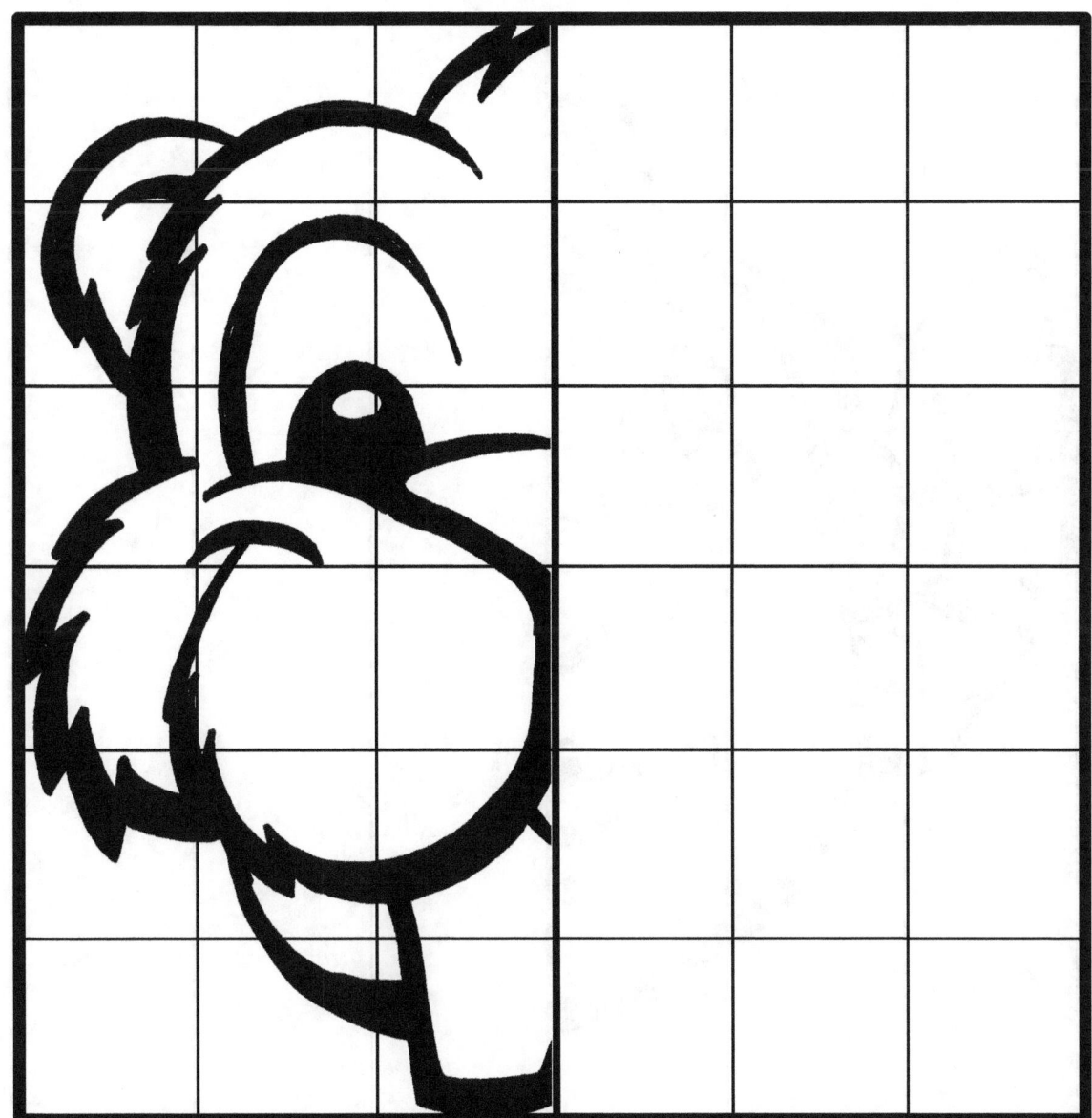

GROUNDHOG

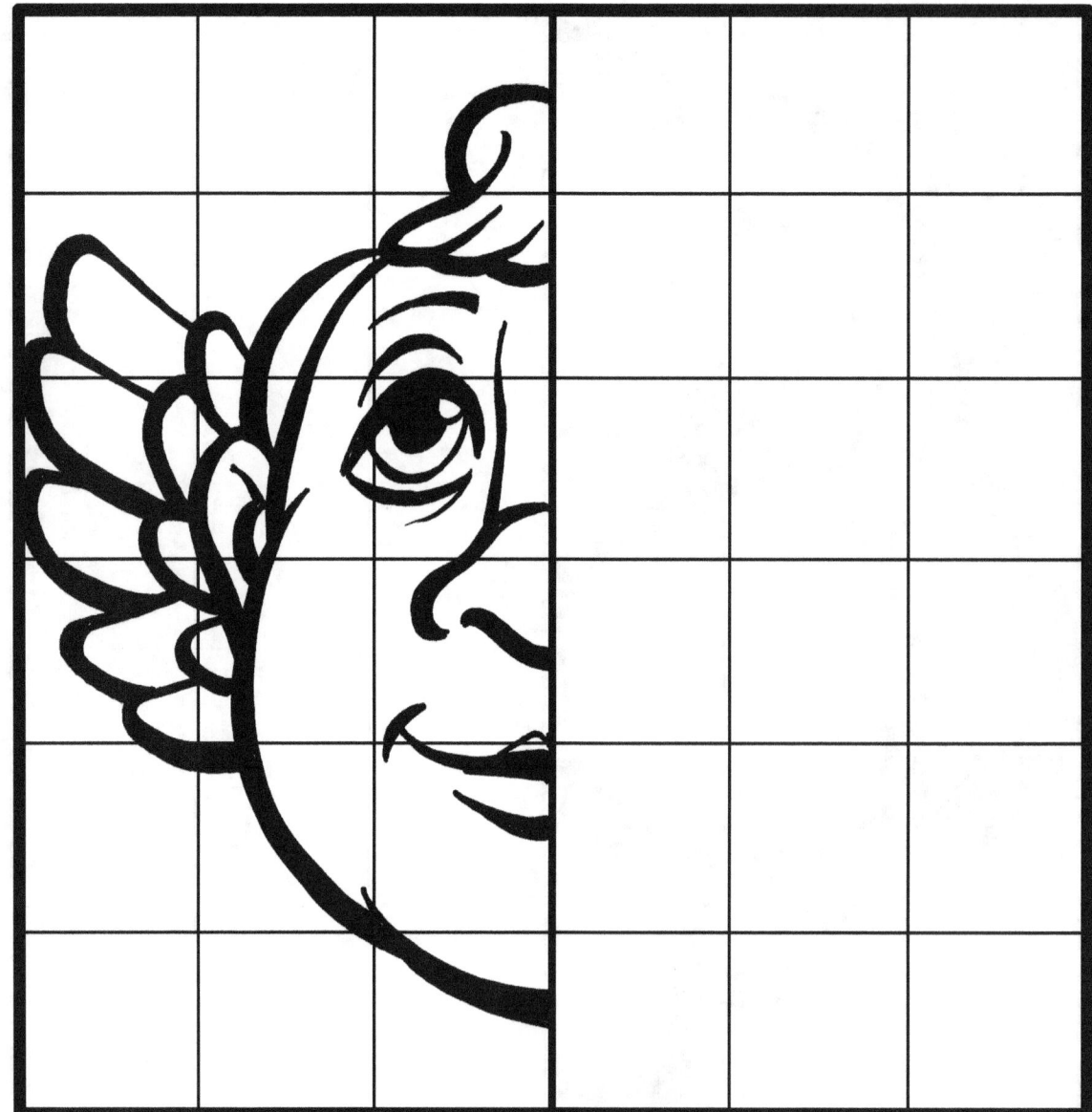

CUPID

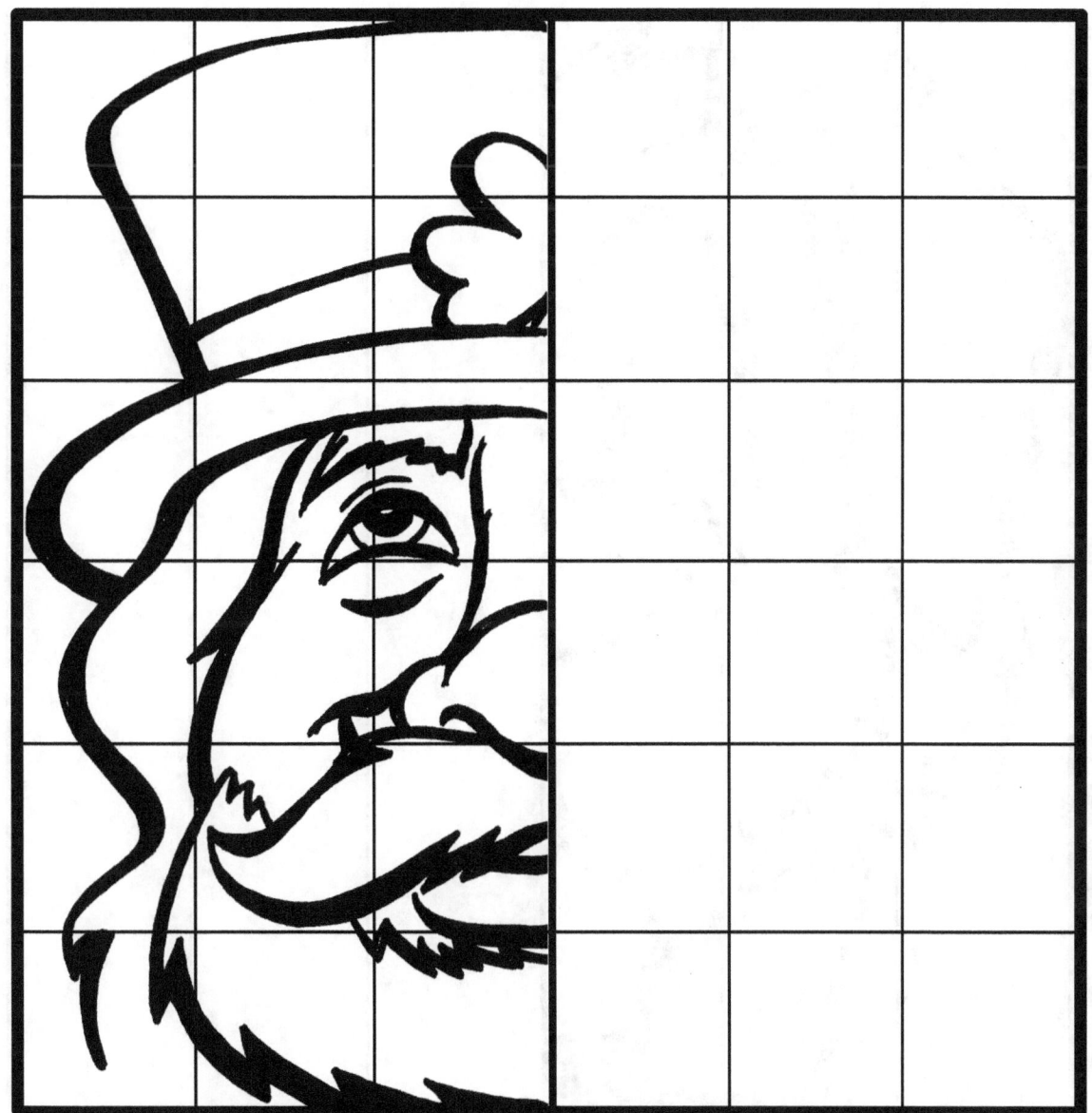

LEPRECHAUN

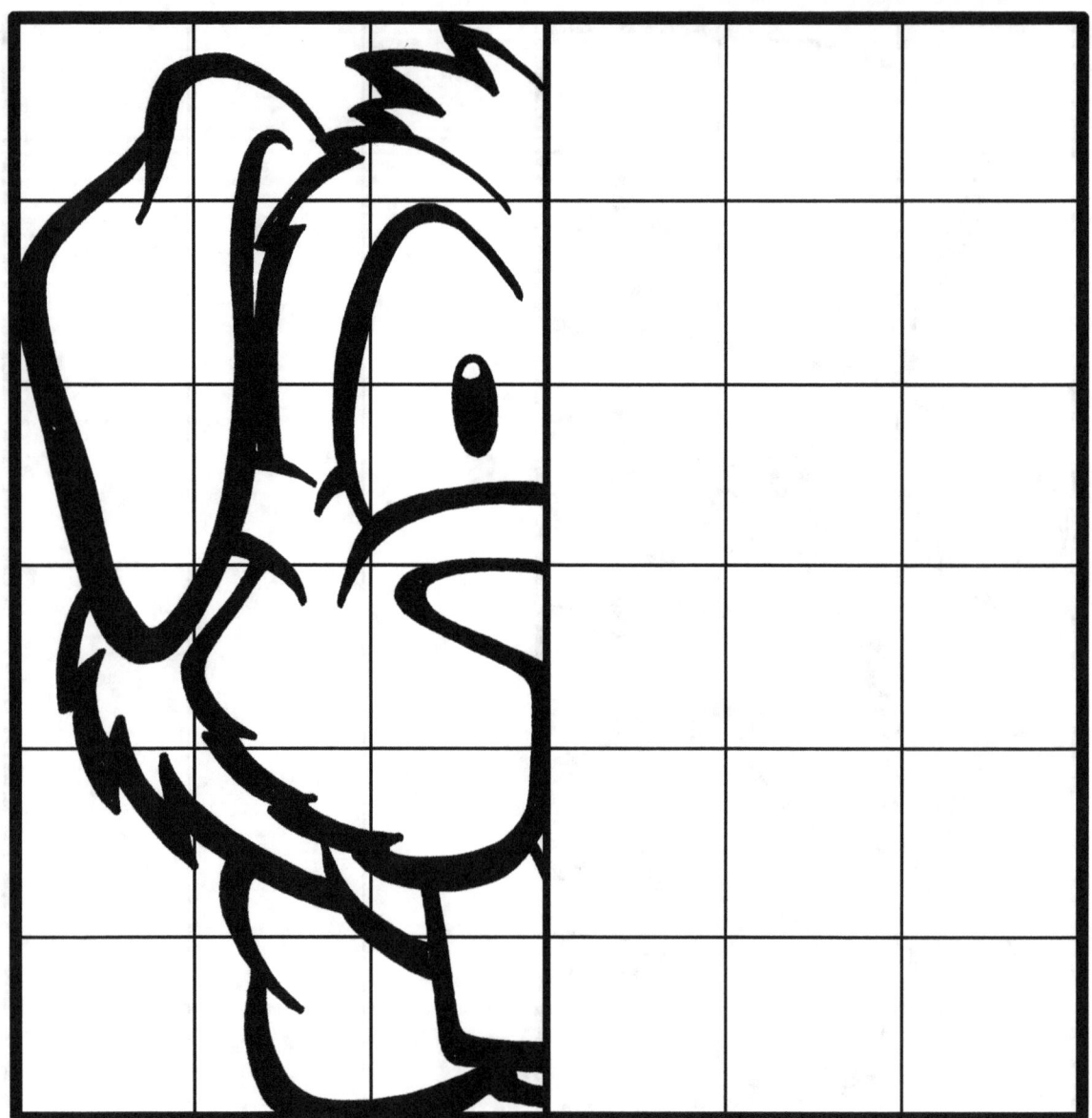

EASTER BUNNY

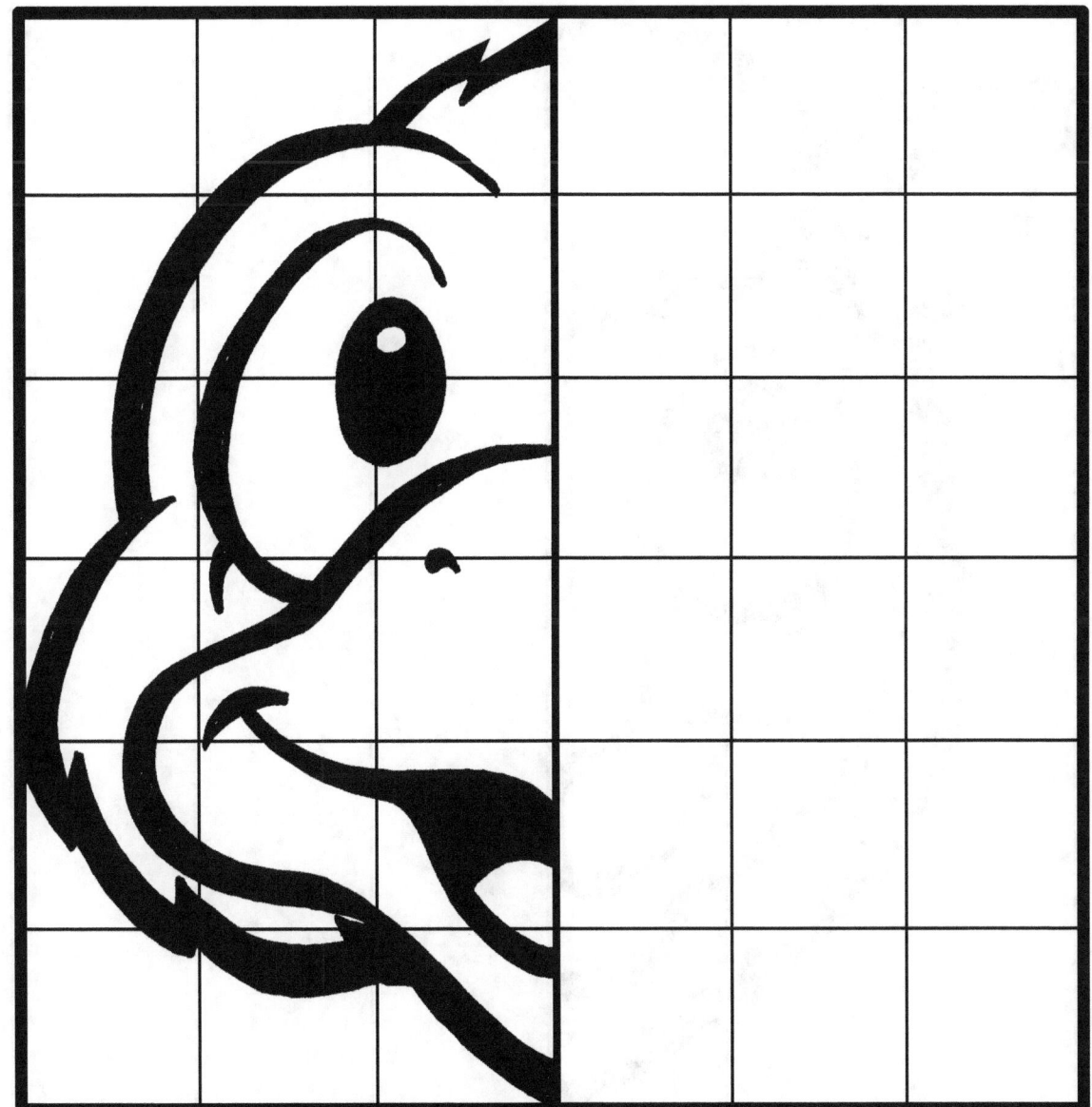

EASTER CHICK

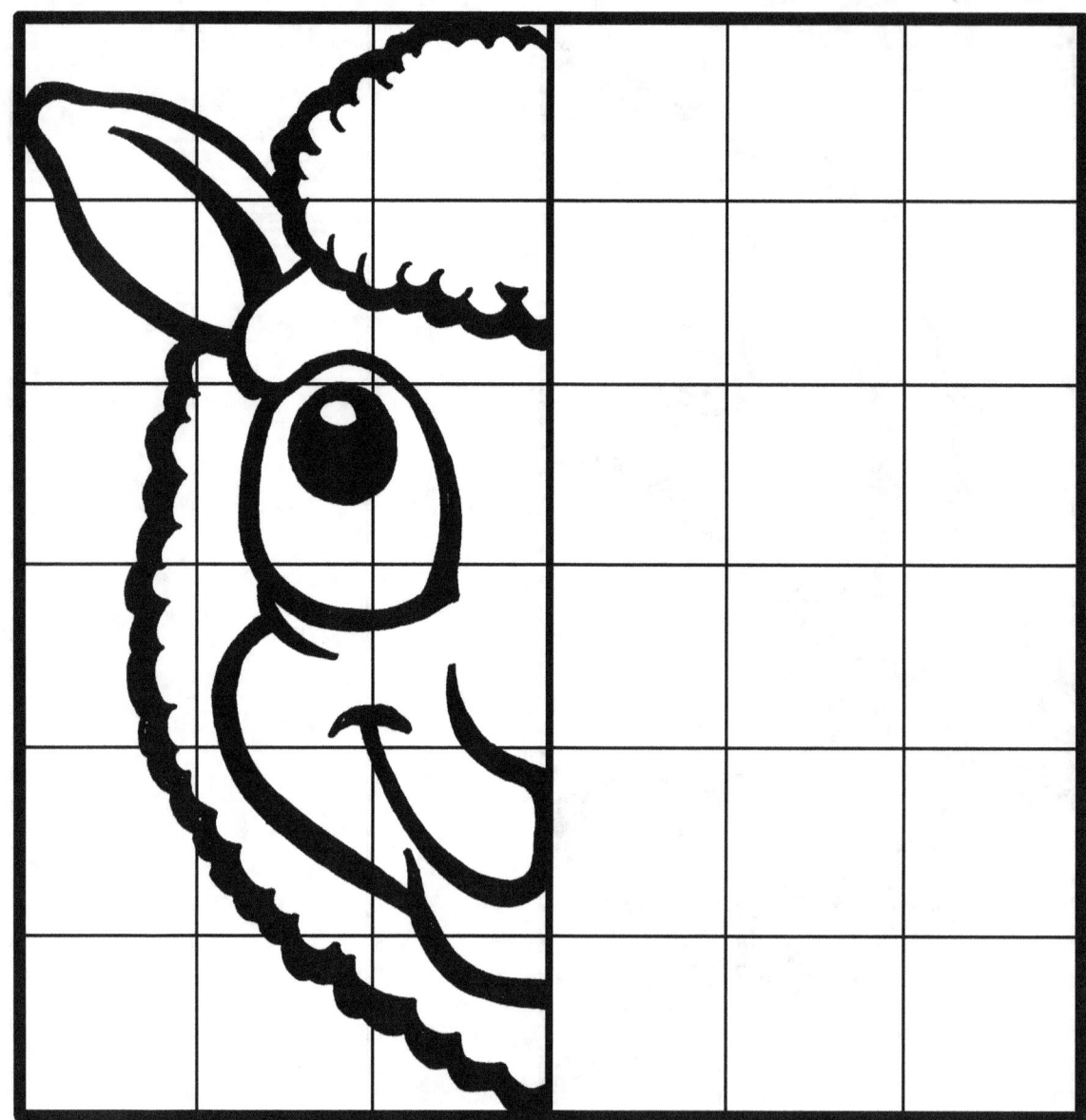

EASTER LAMB

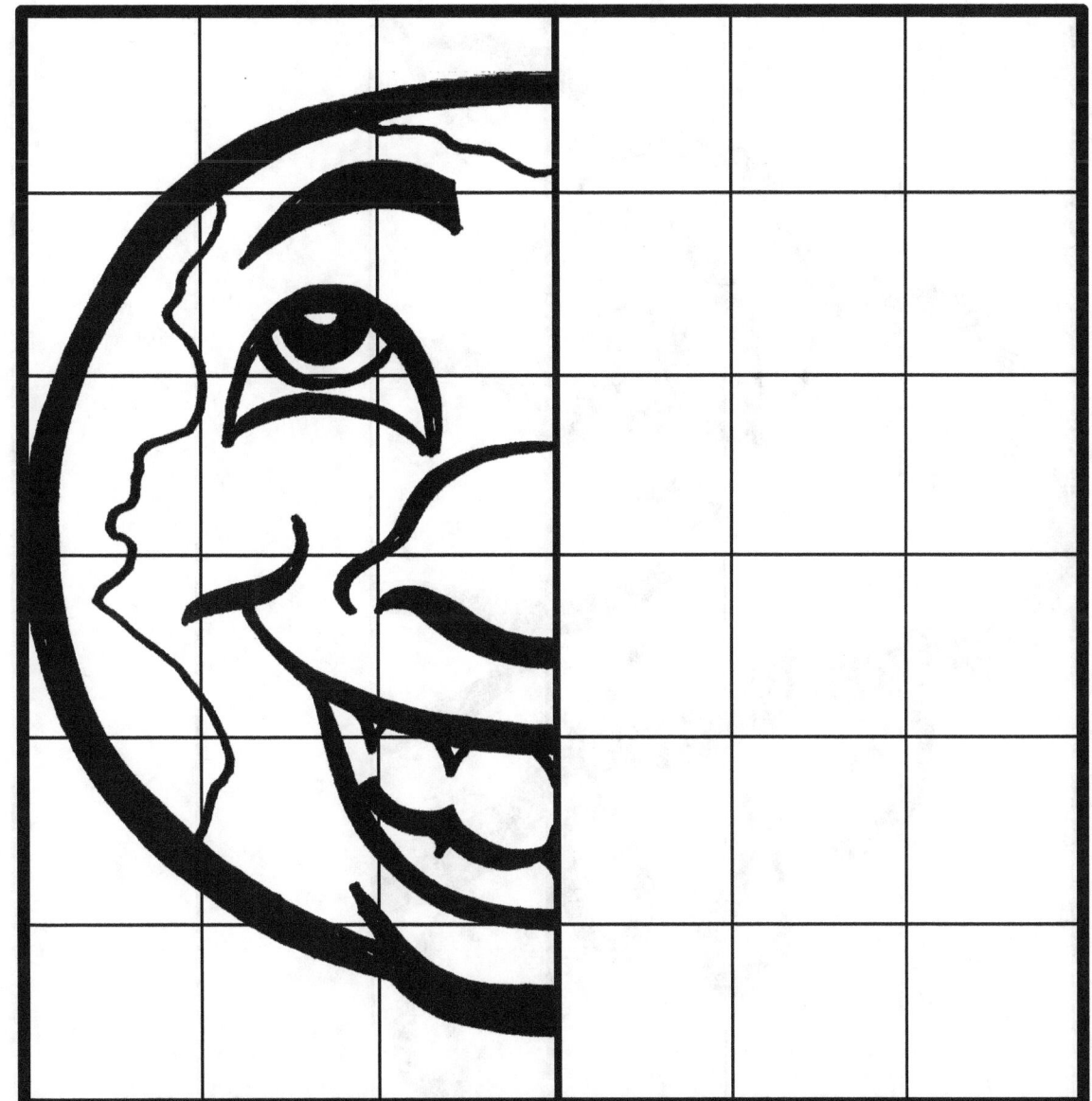

EARTH DAY

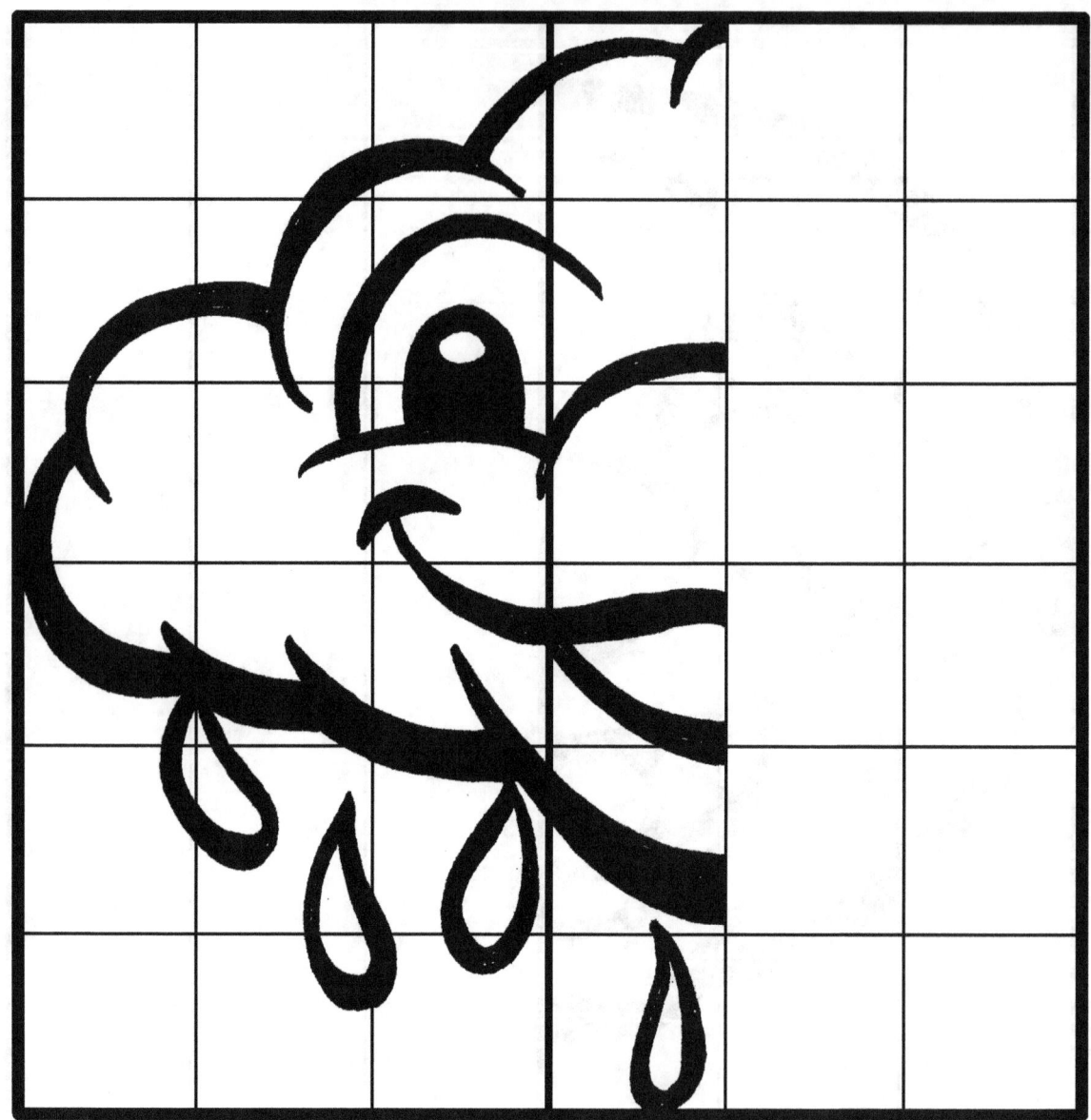

April Showers

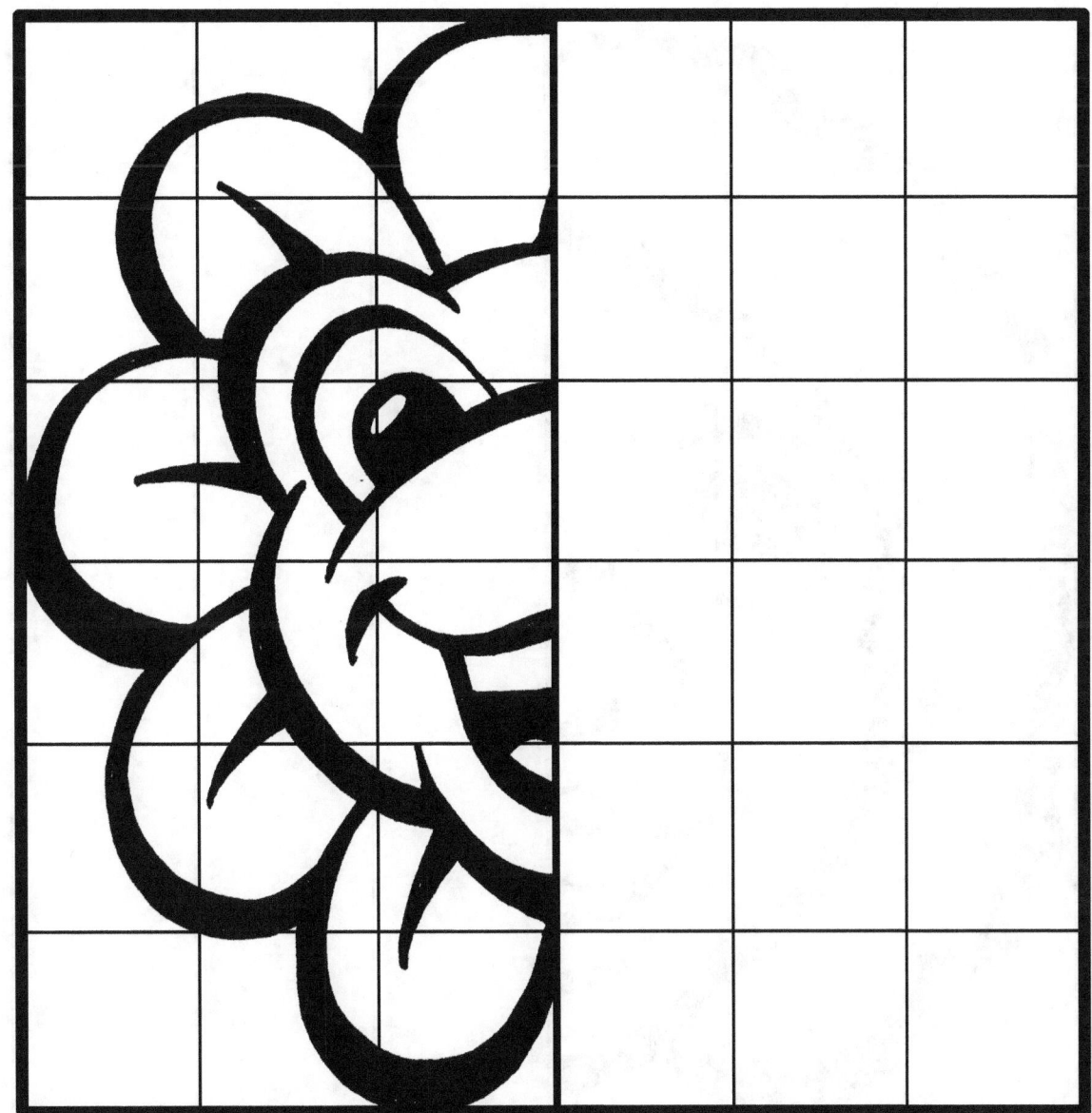

MAY FLOWERS

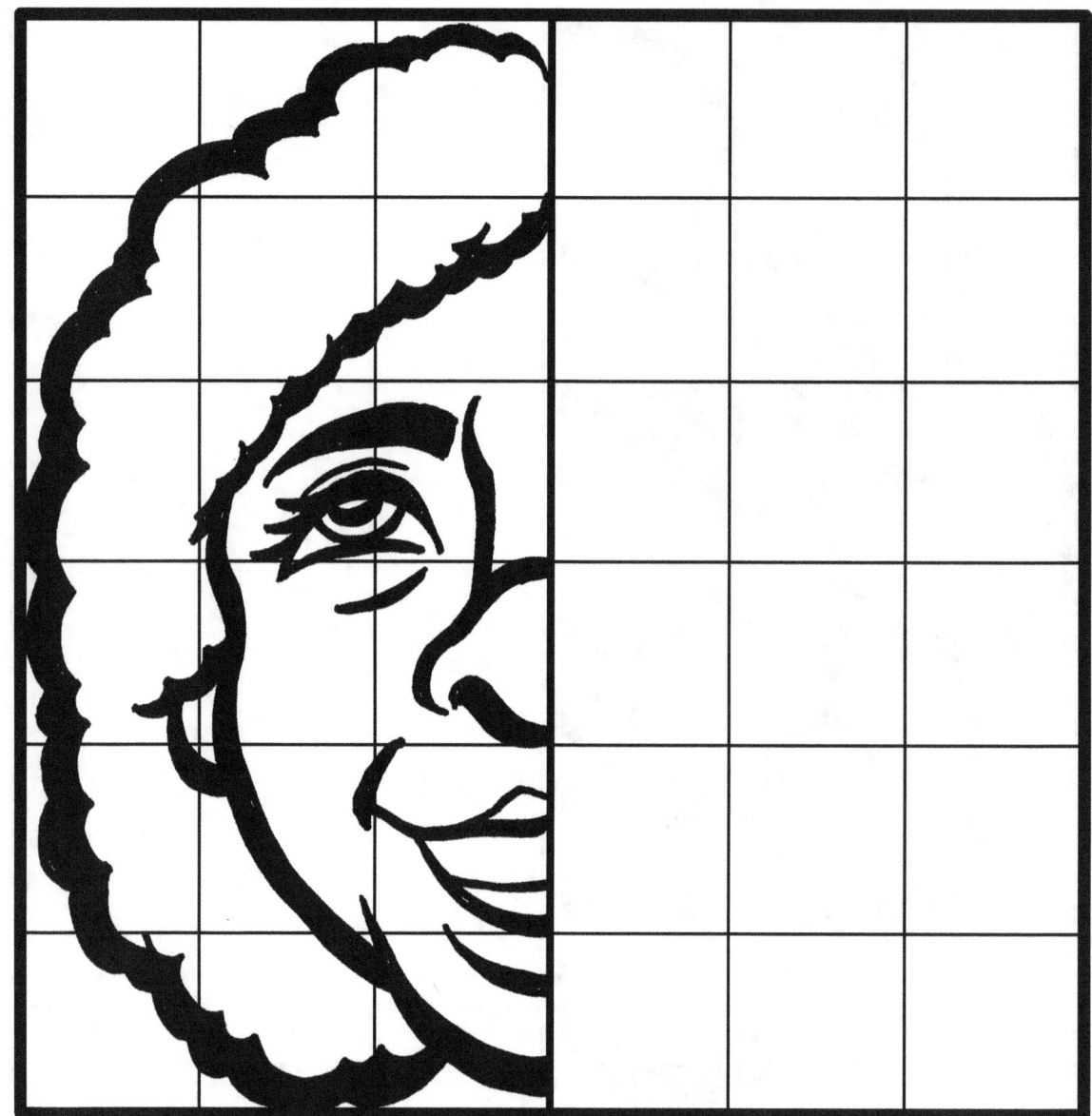

MOTHERS DAY

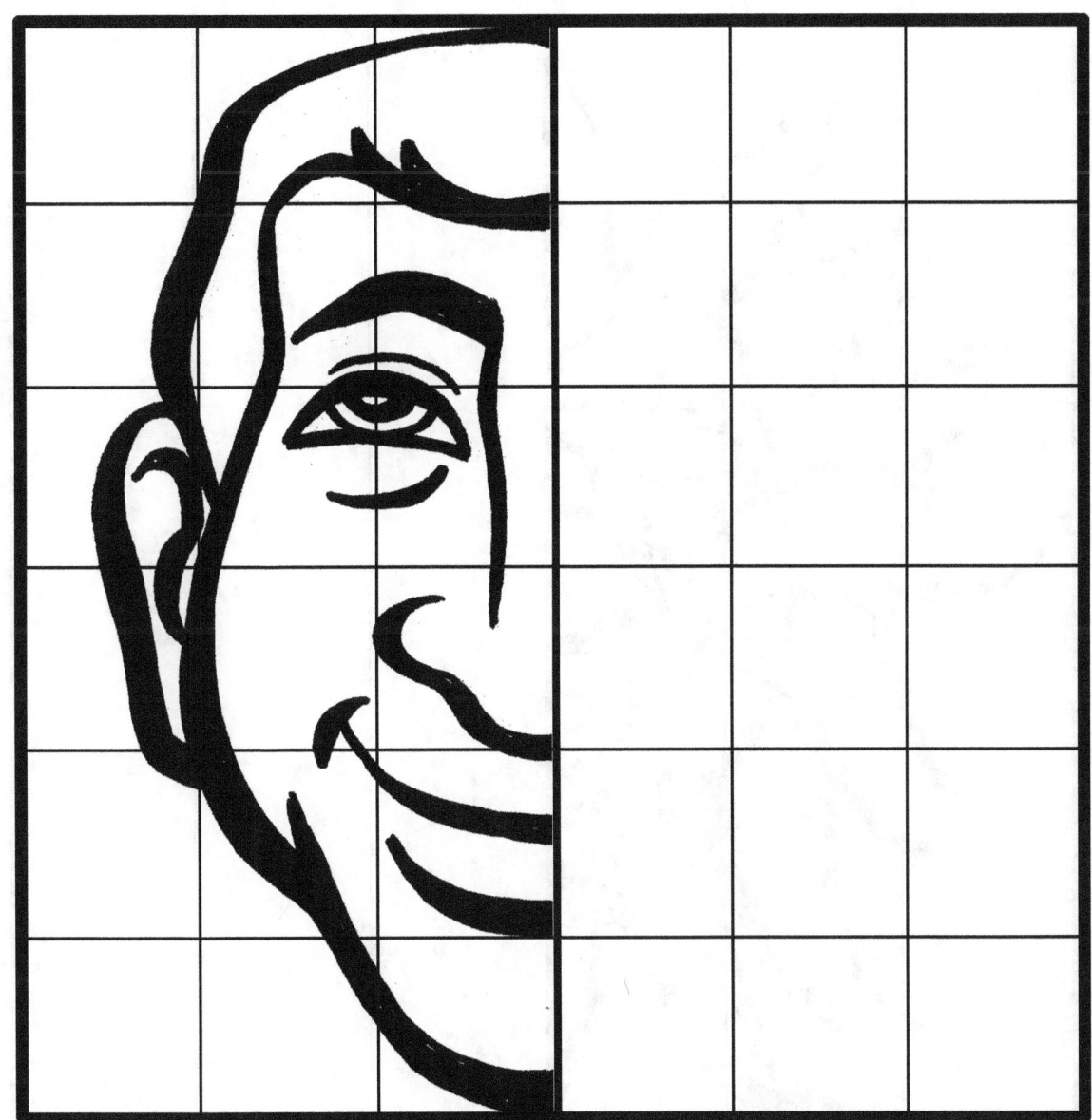

FATHERS DAY

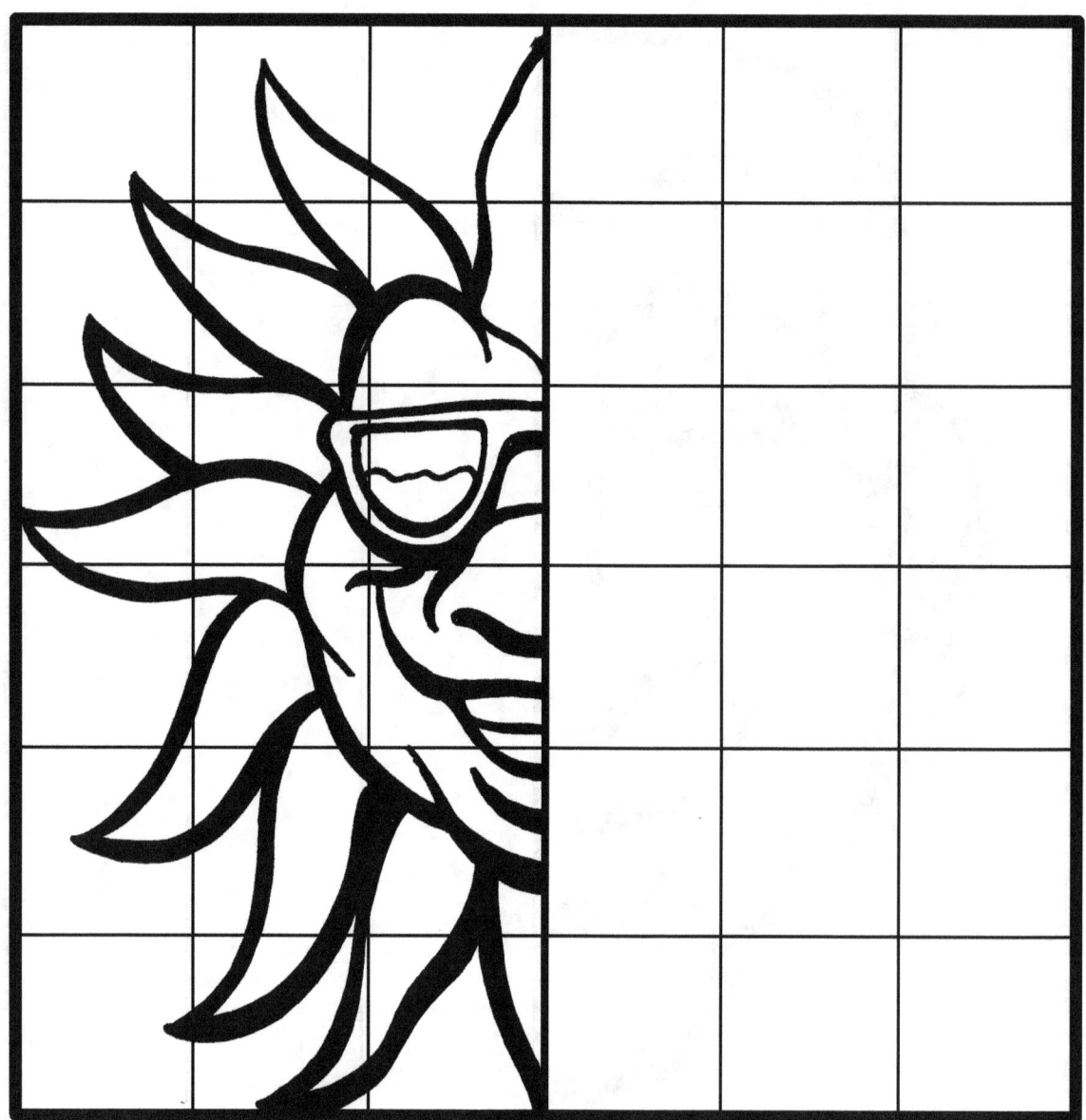

SUMMER SUN

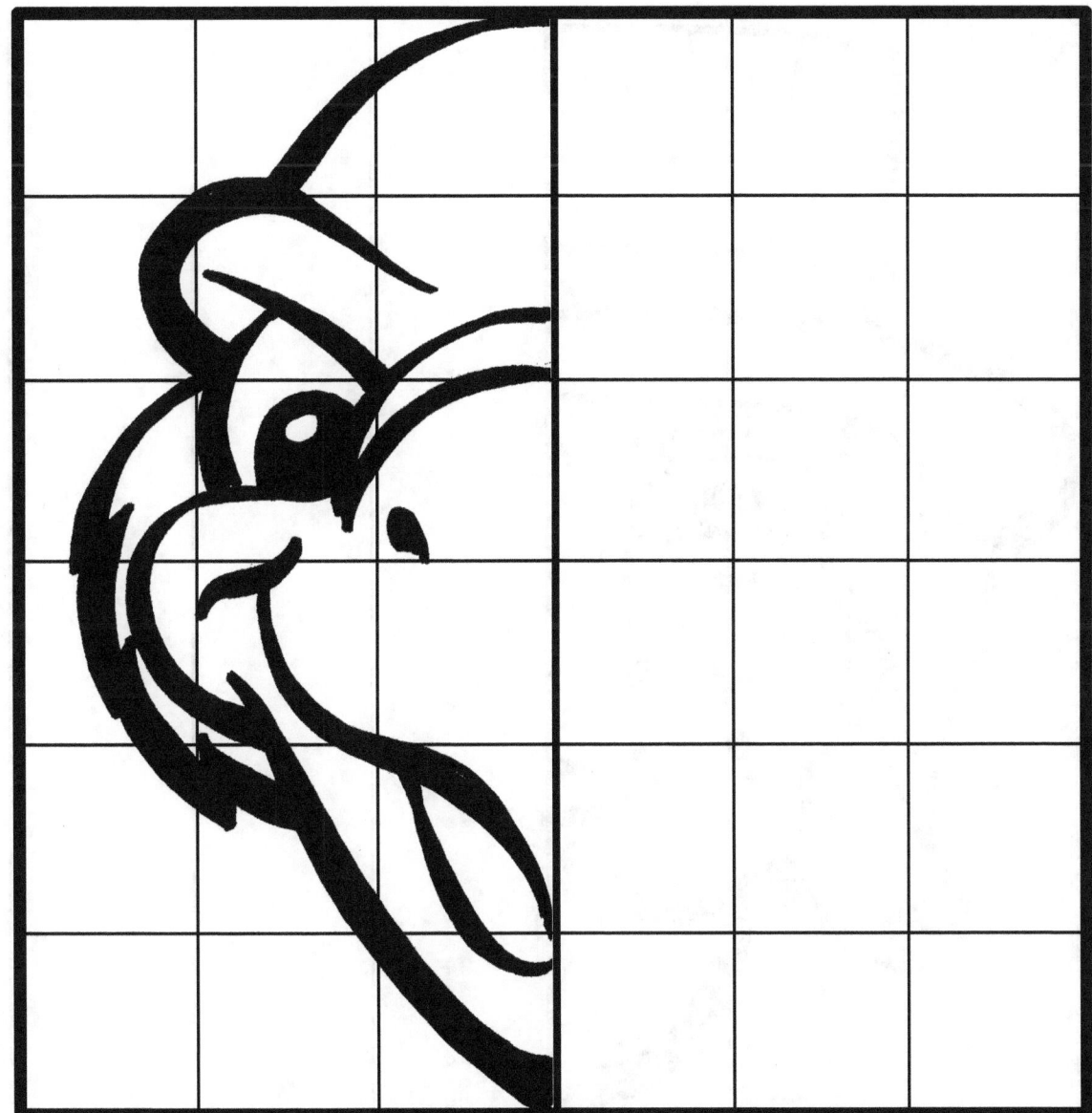

AMERICAN EAGLE

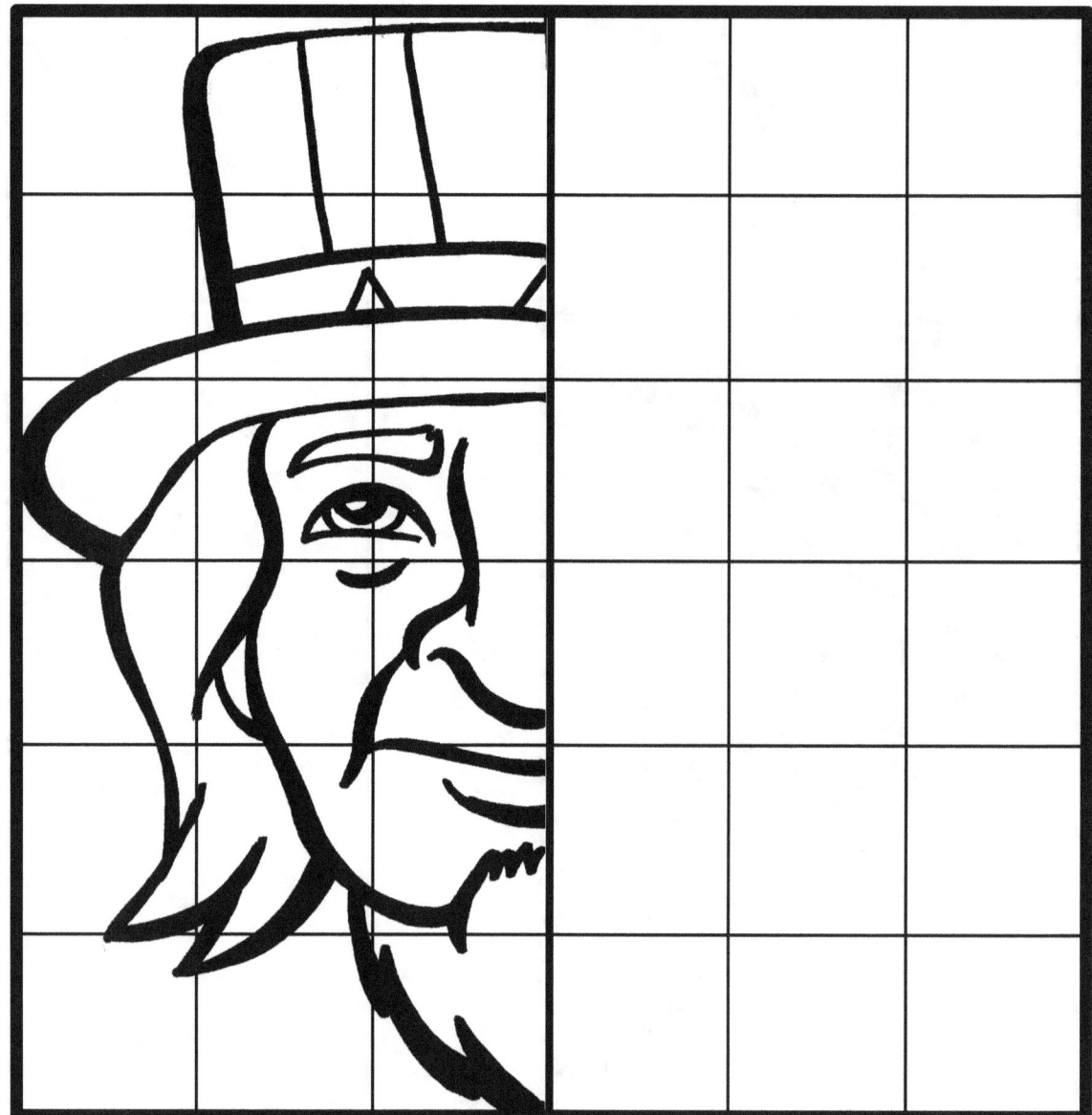

UNCLE SAM

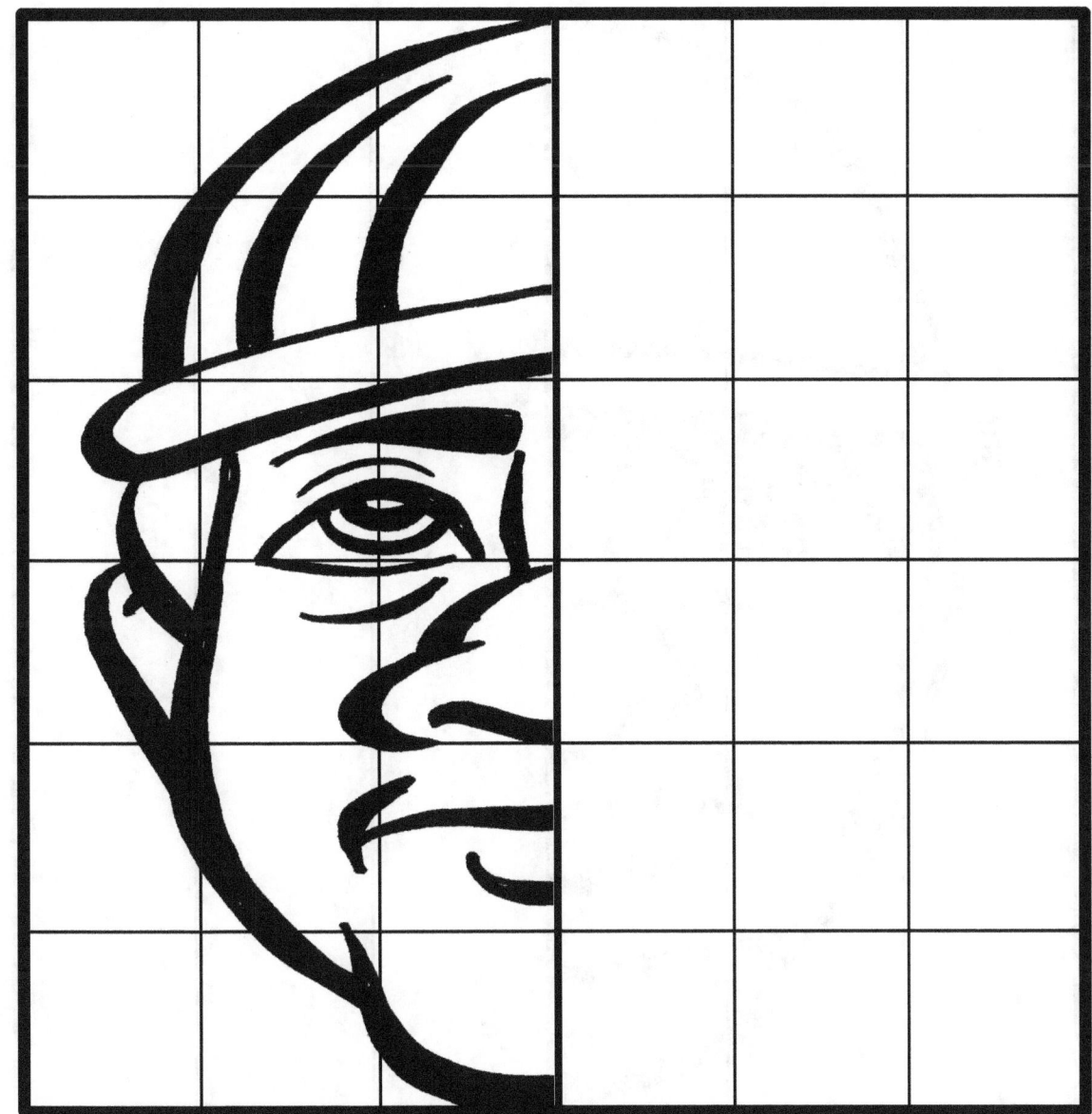

LABOR DAY

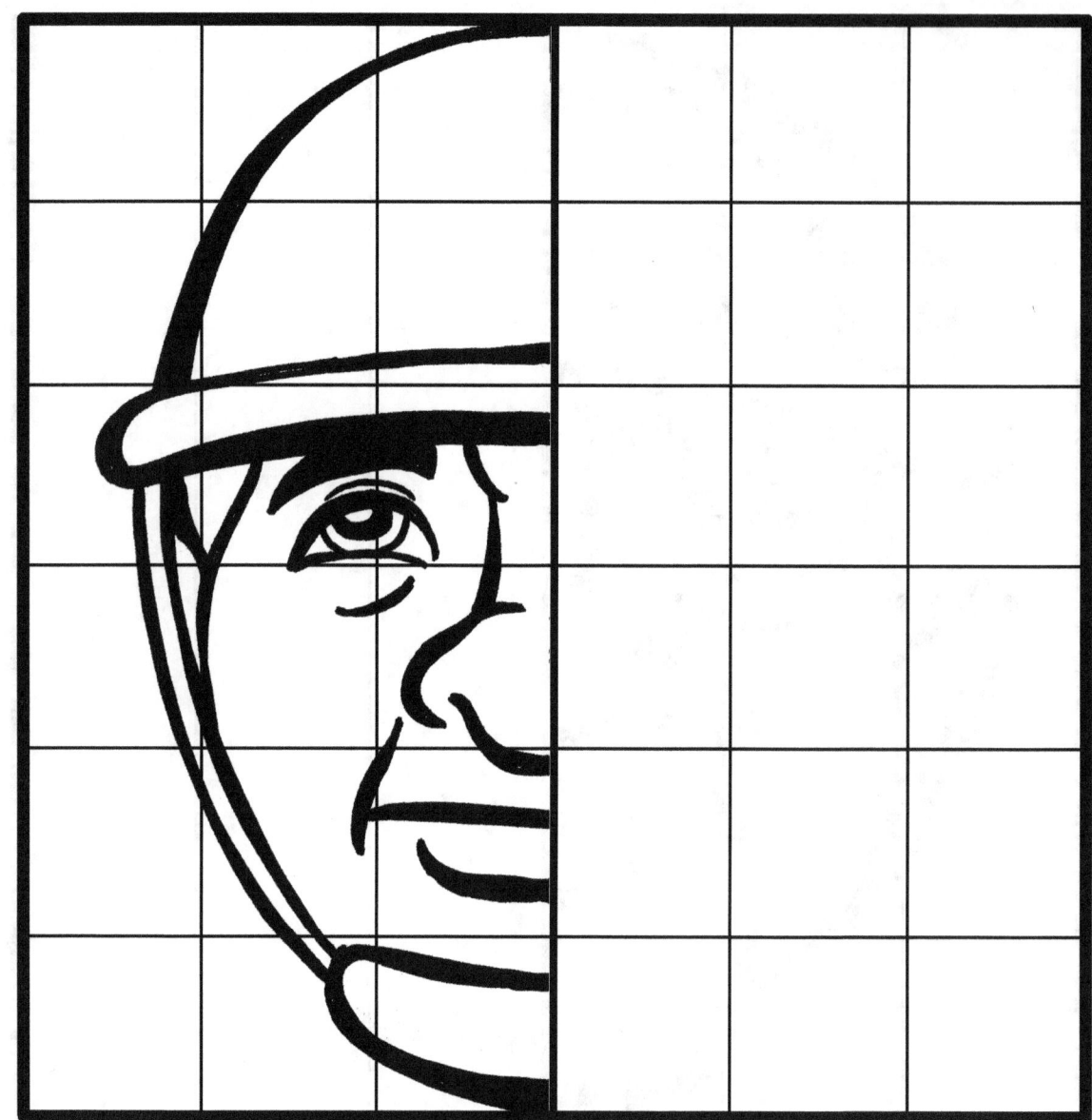

VETERANS DAY

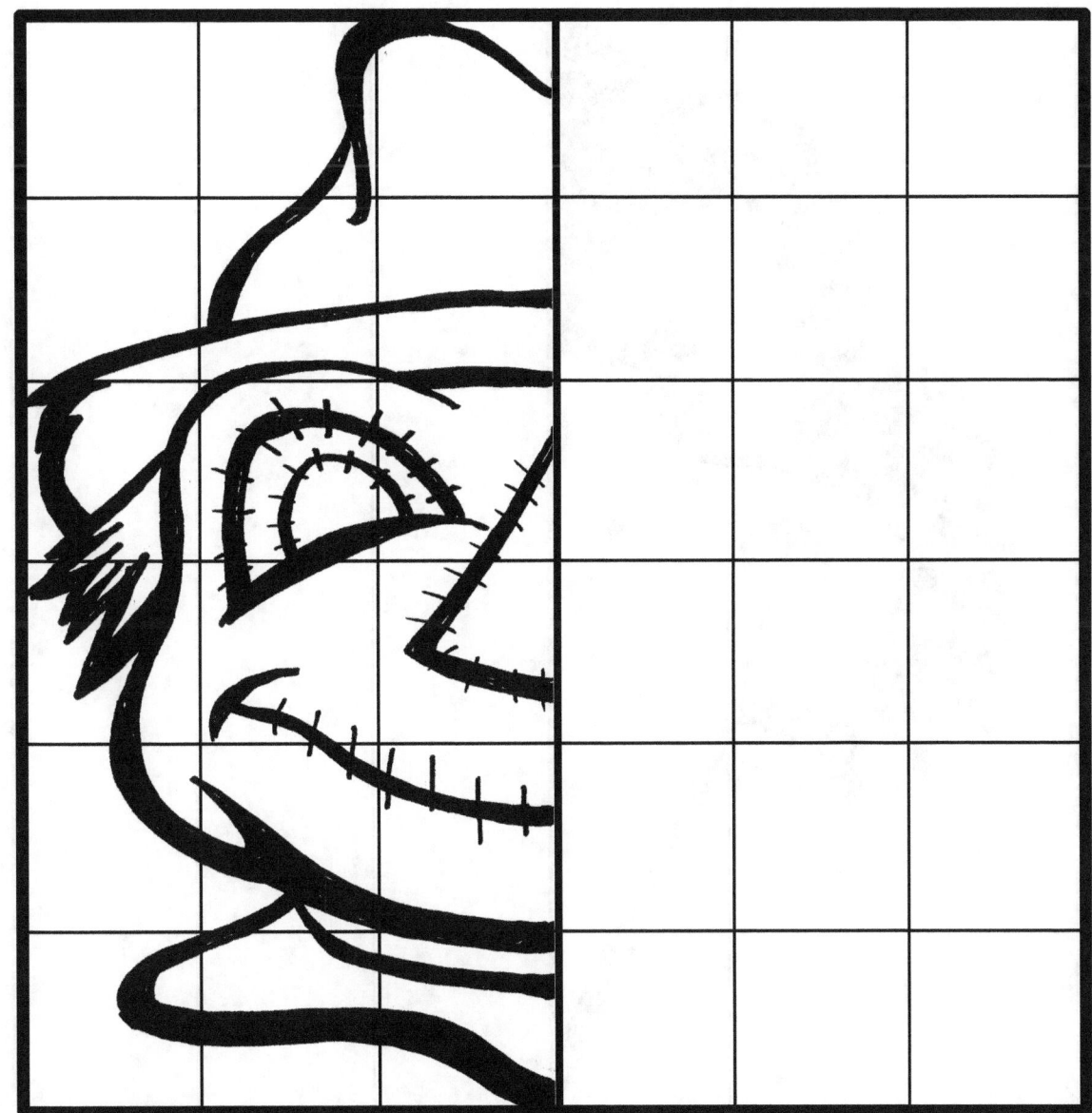

SCARECROW

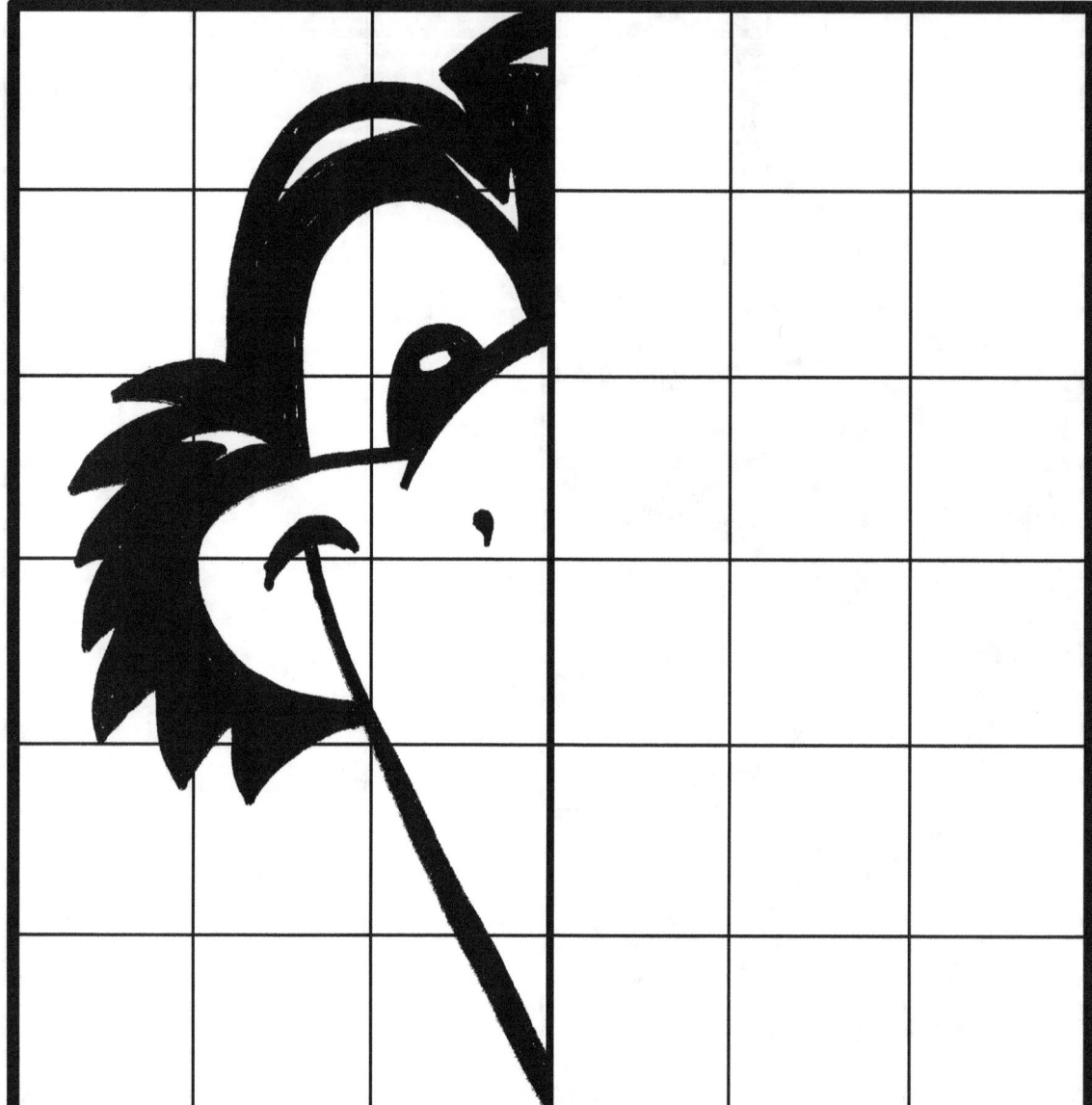

CROW

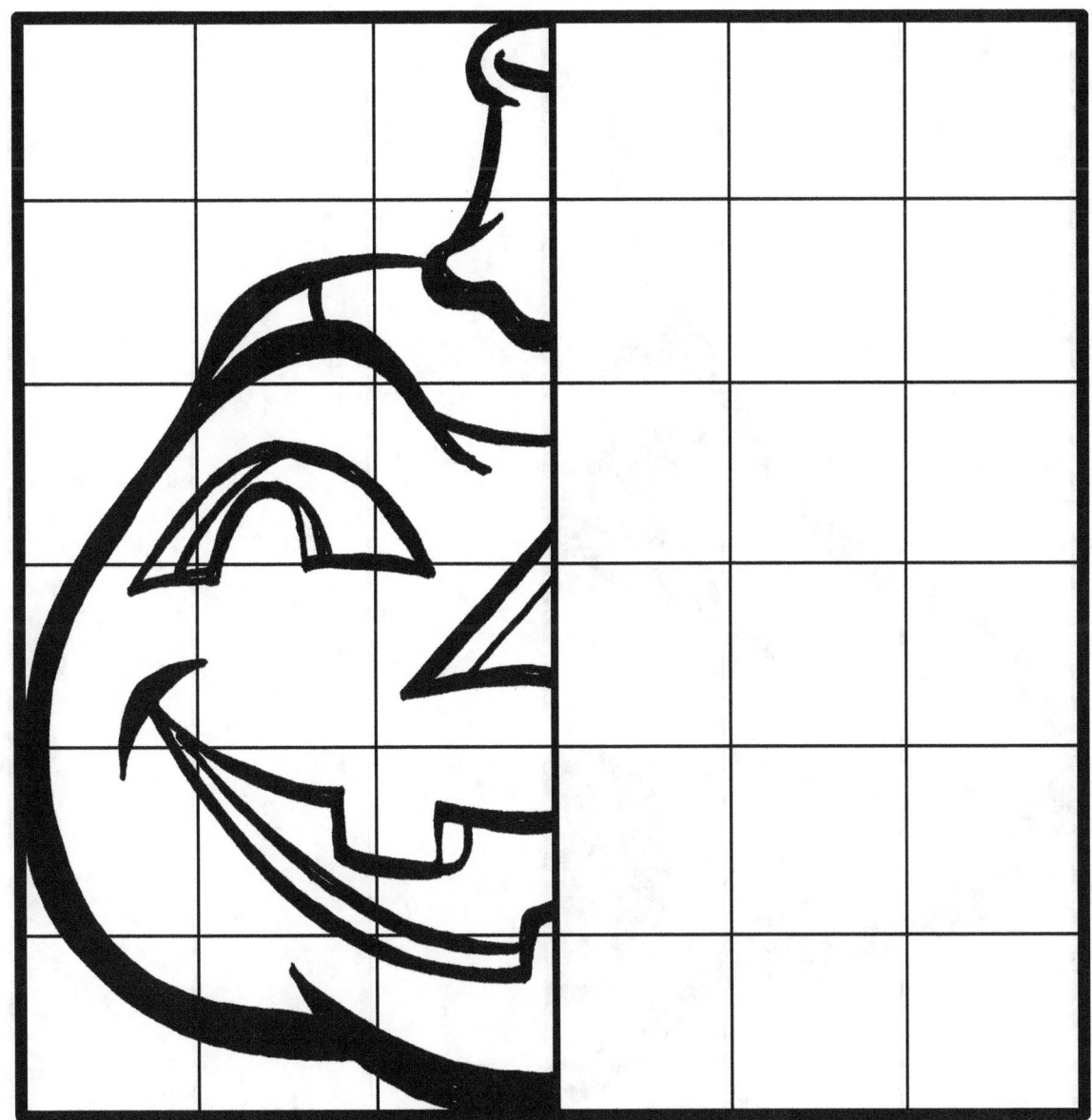

JACK-O

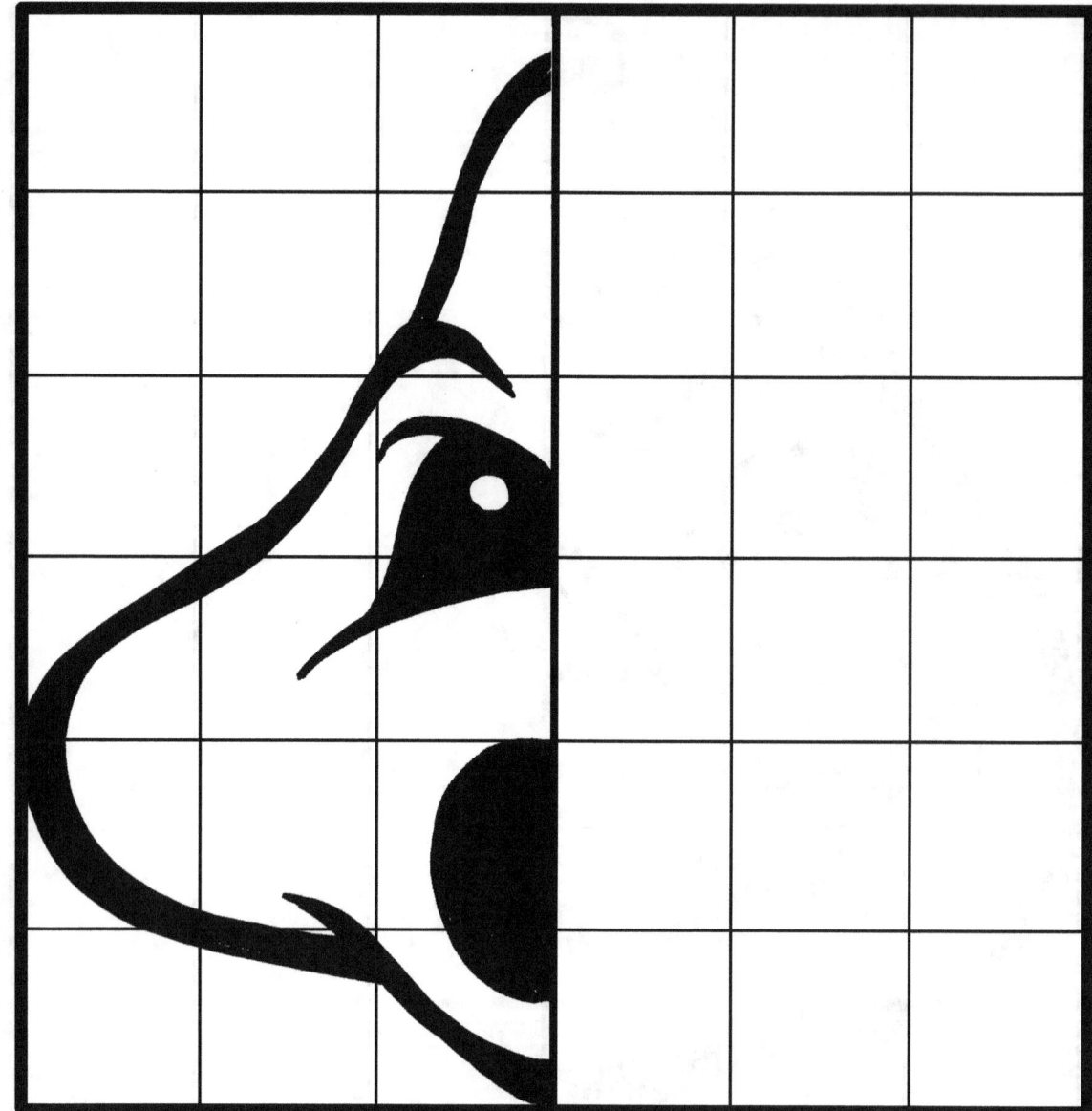

SPOOKER

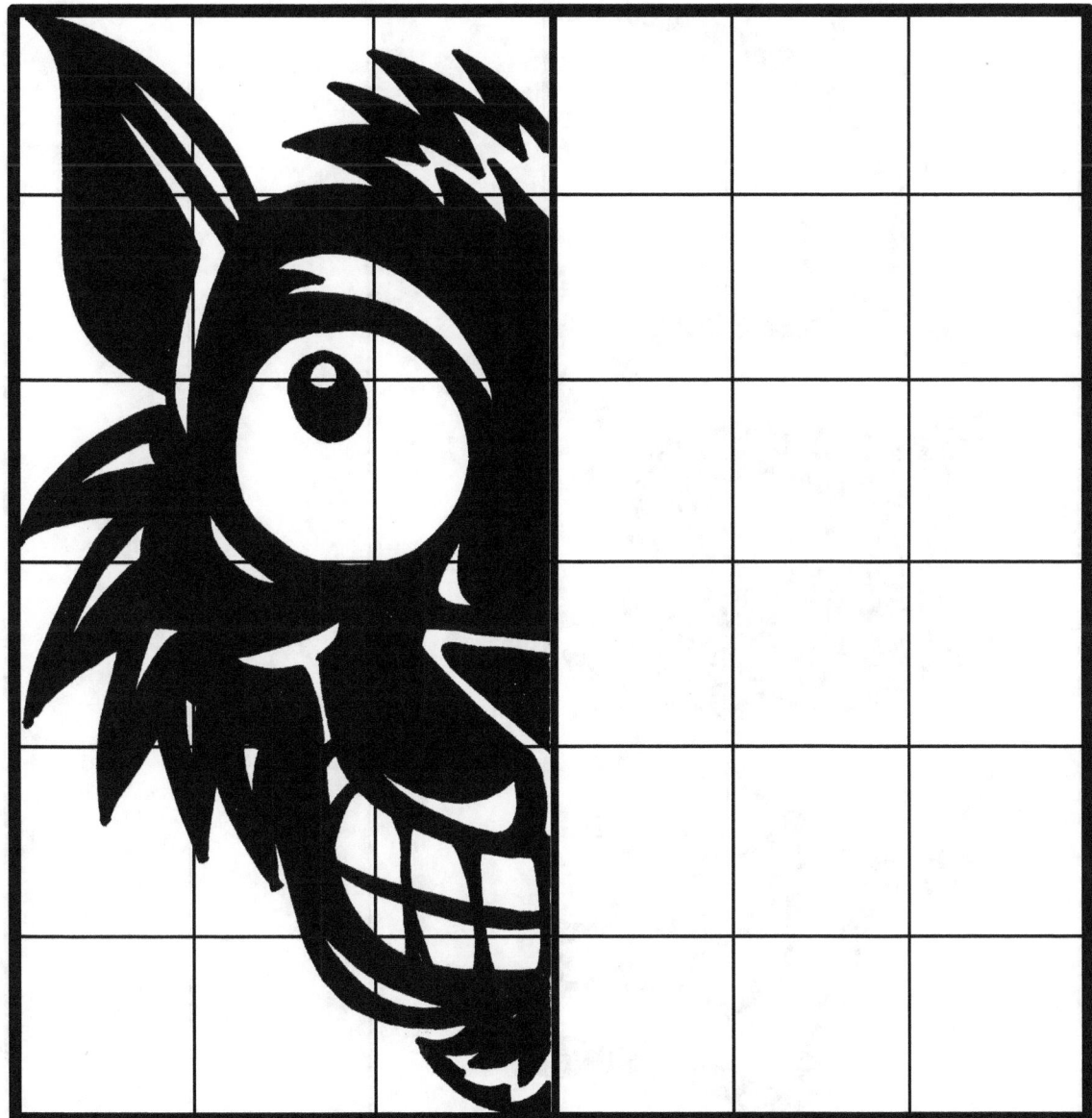

BLACK CAT

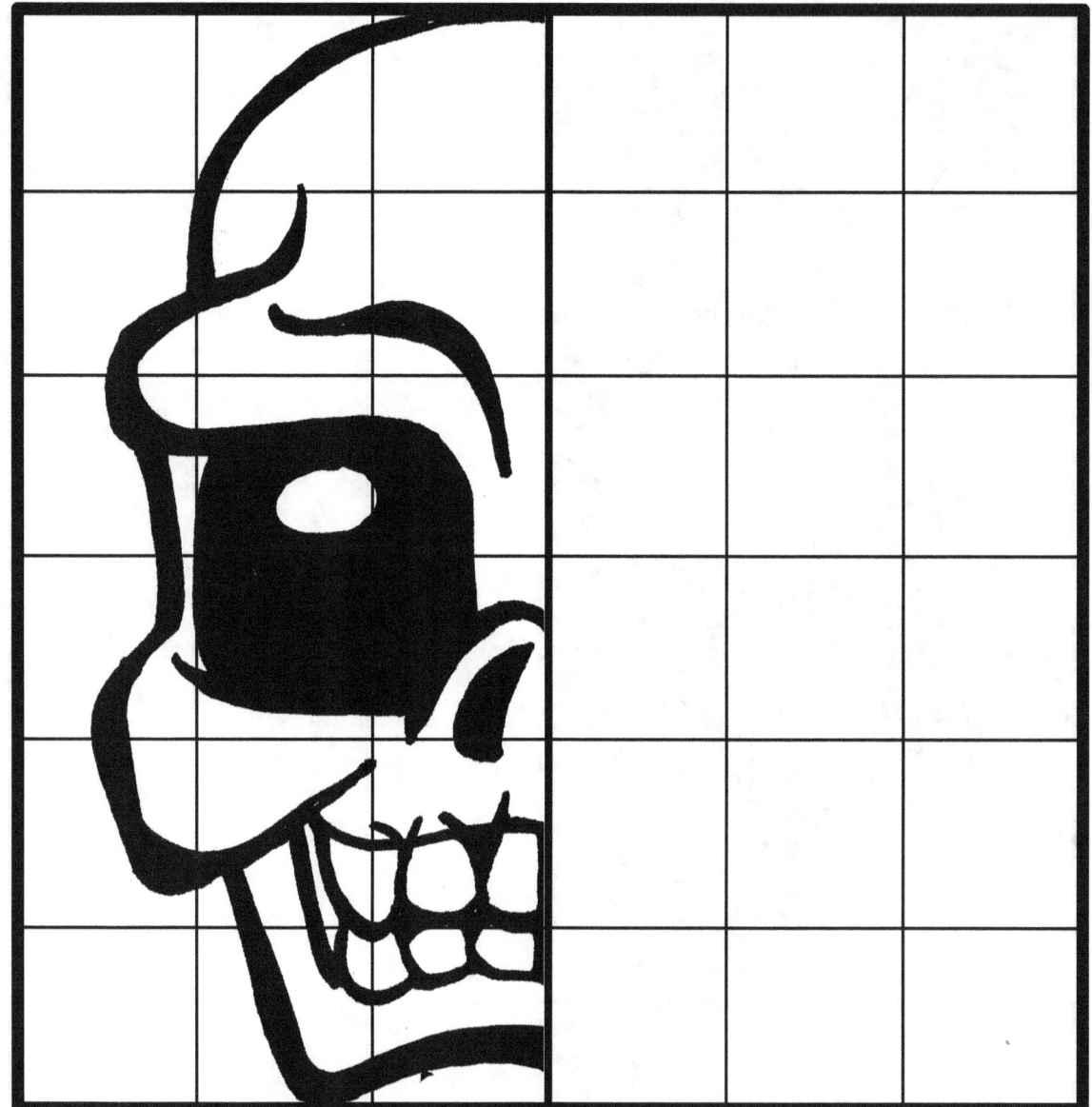

SKELETON

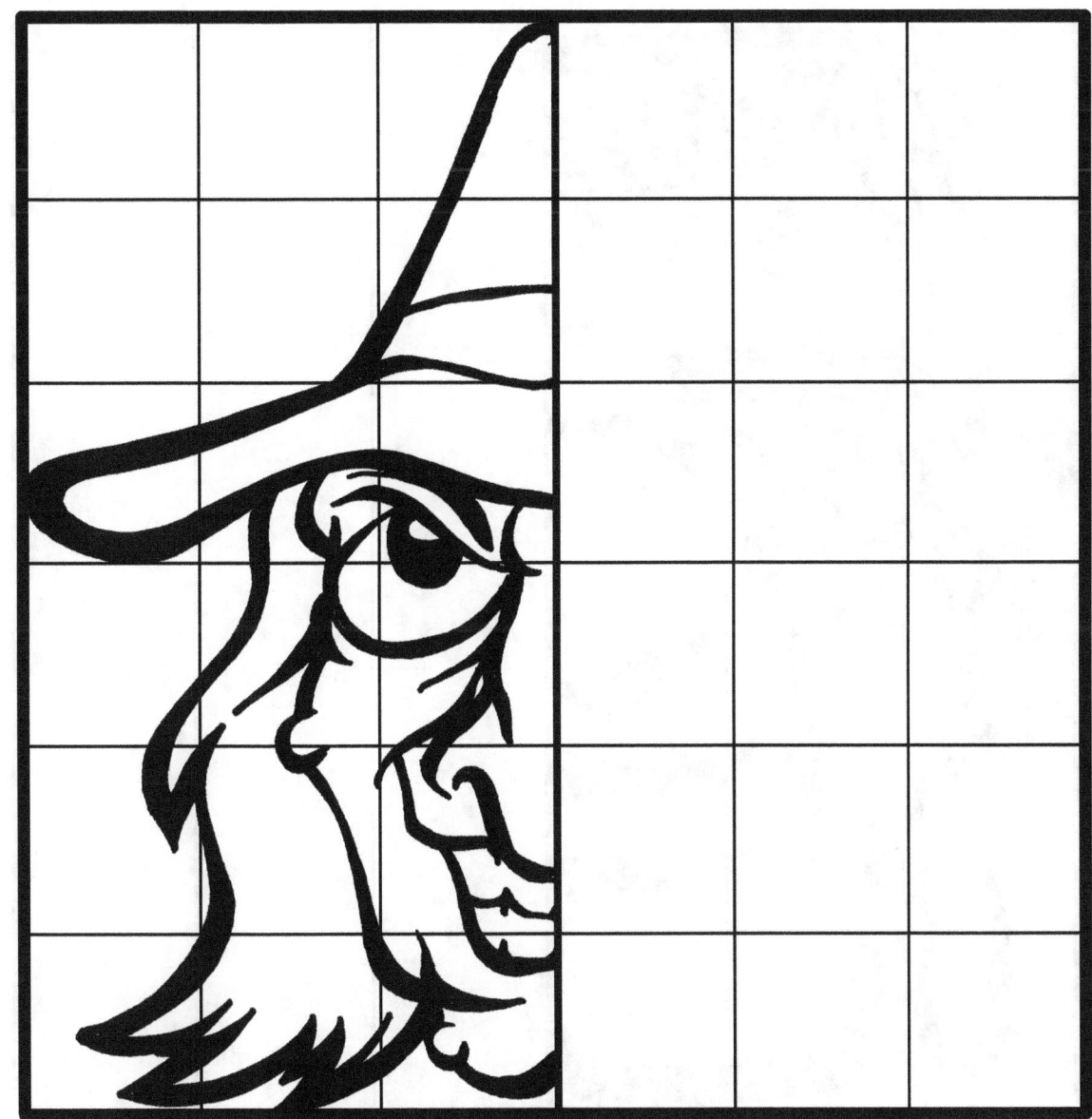

WICKED WITCH

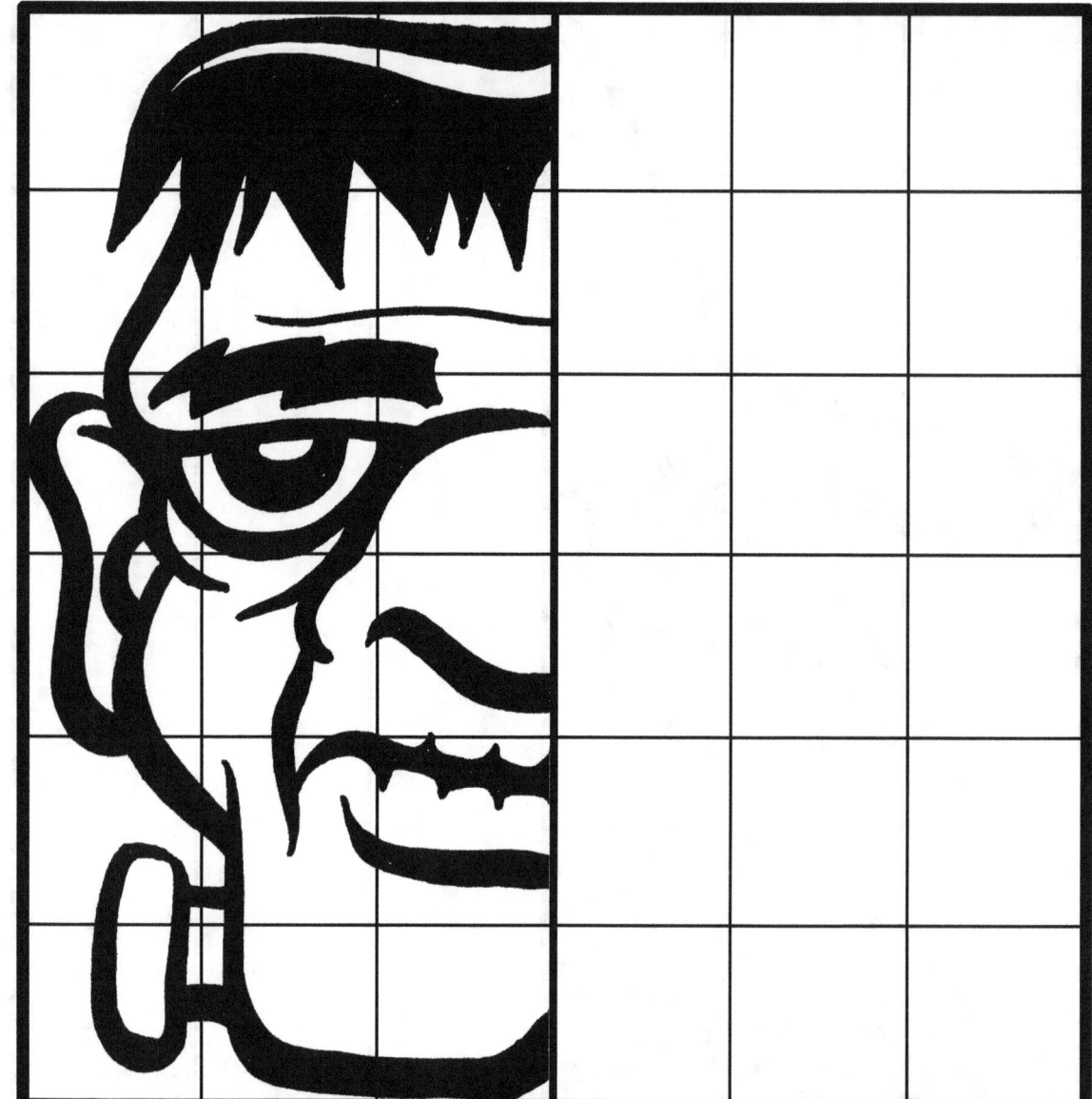

FRANK

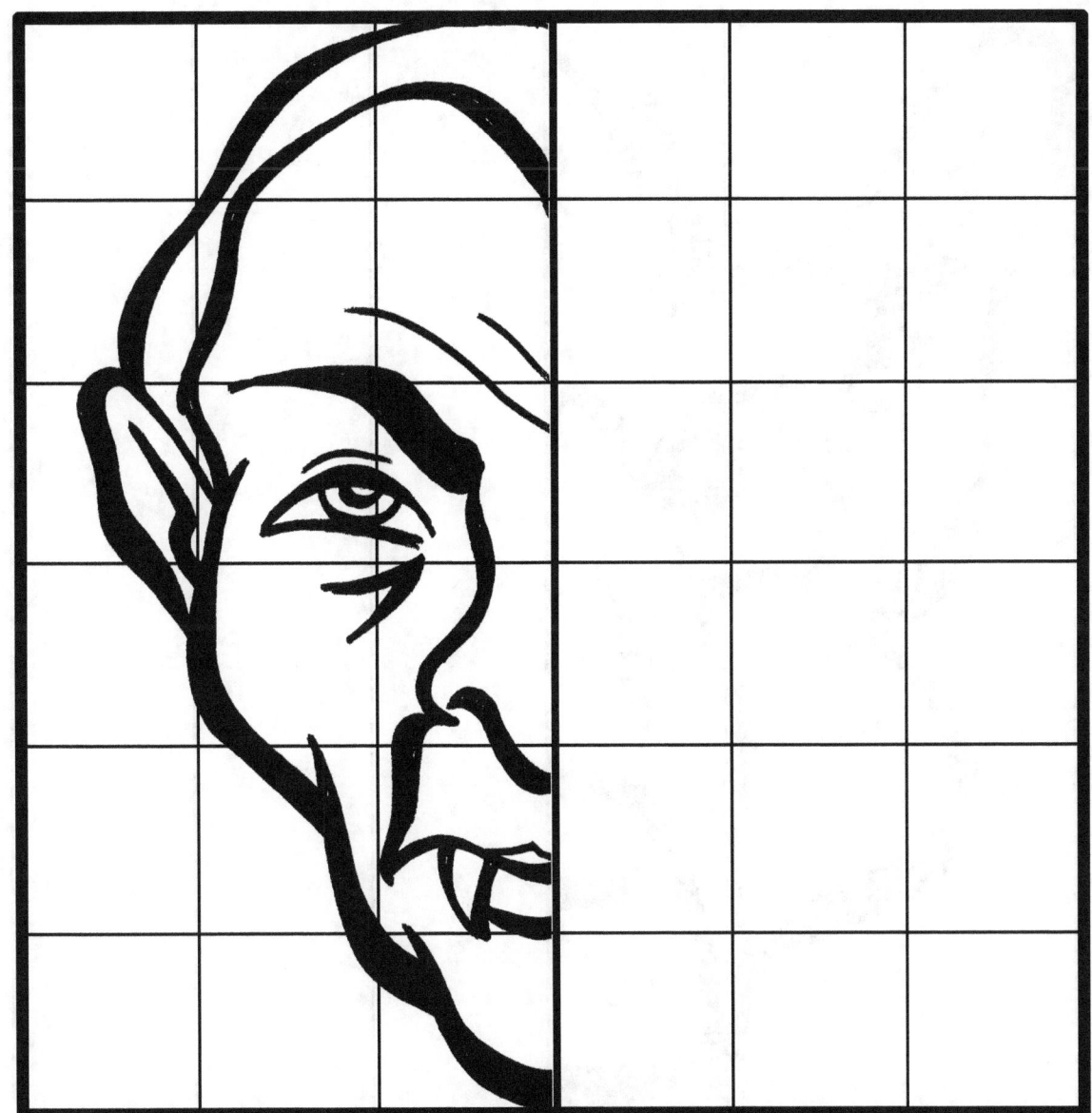

DRACULA

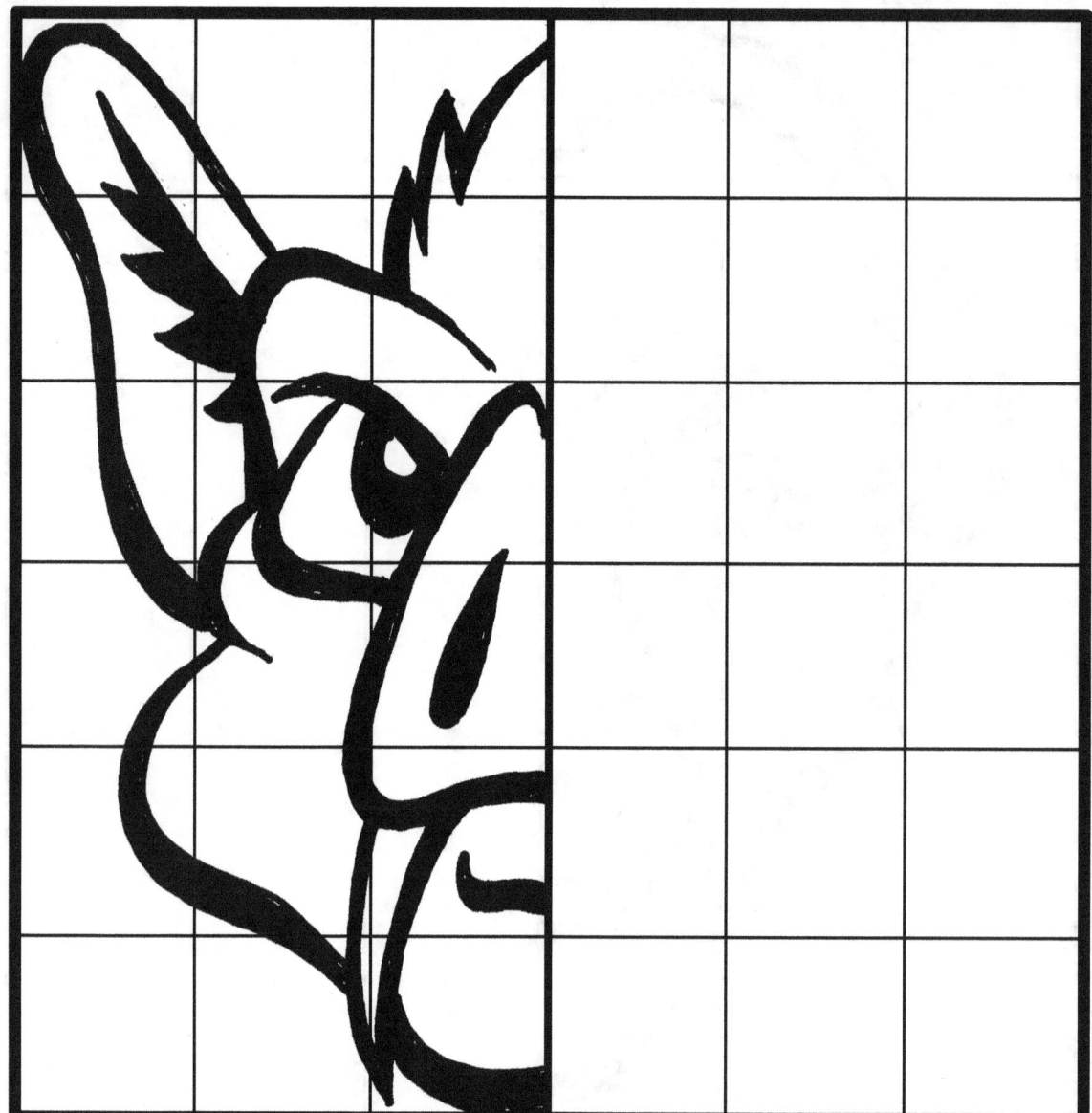

VAMPIRE BAT

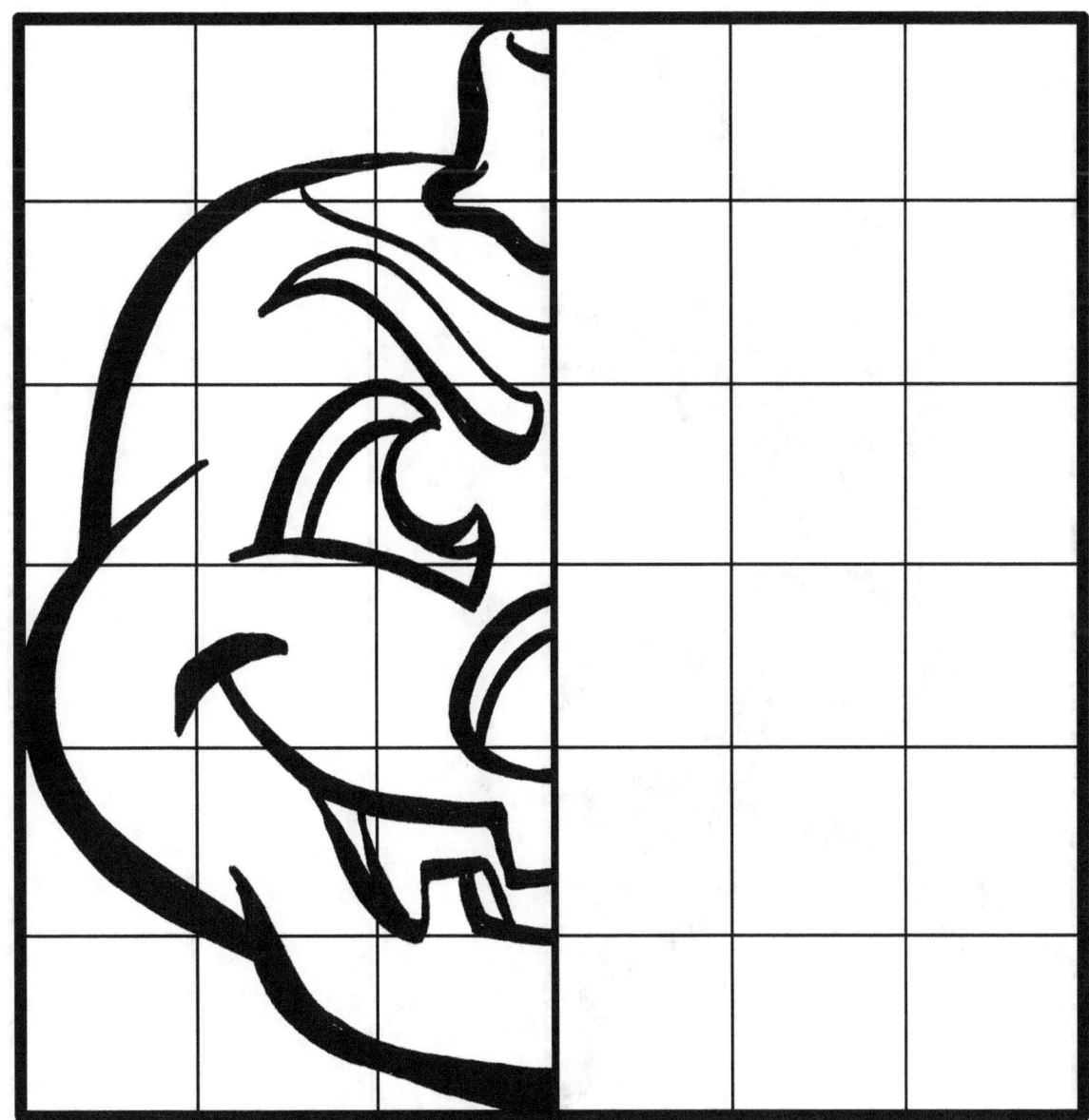

JACK-E LANTERN

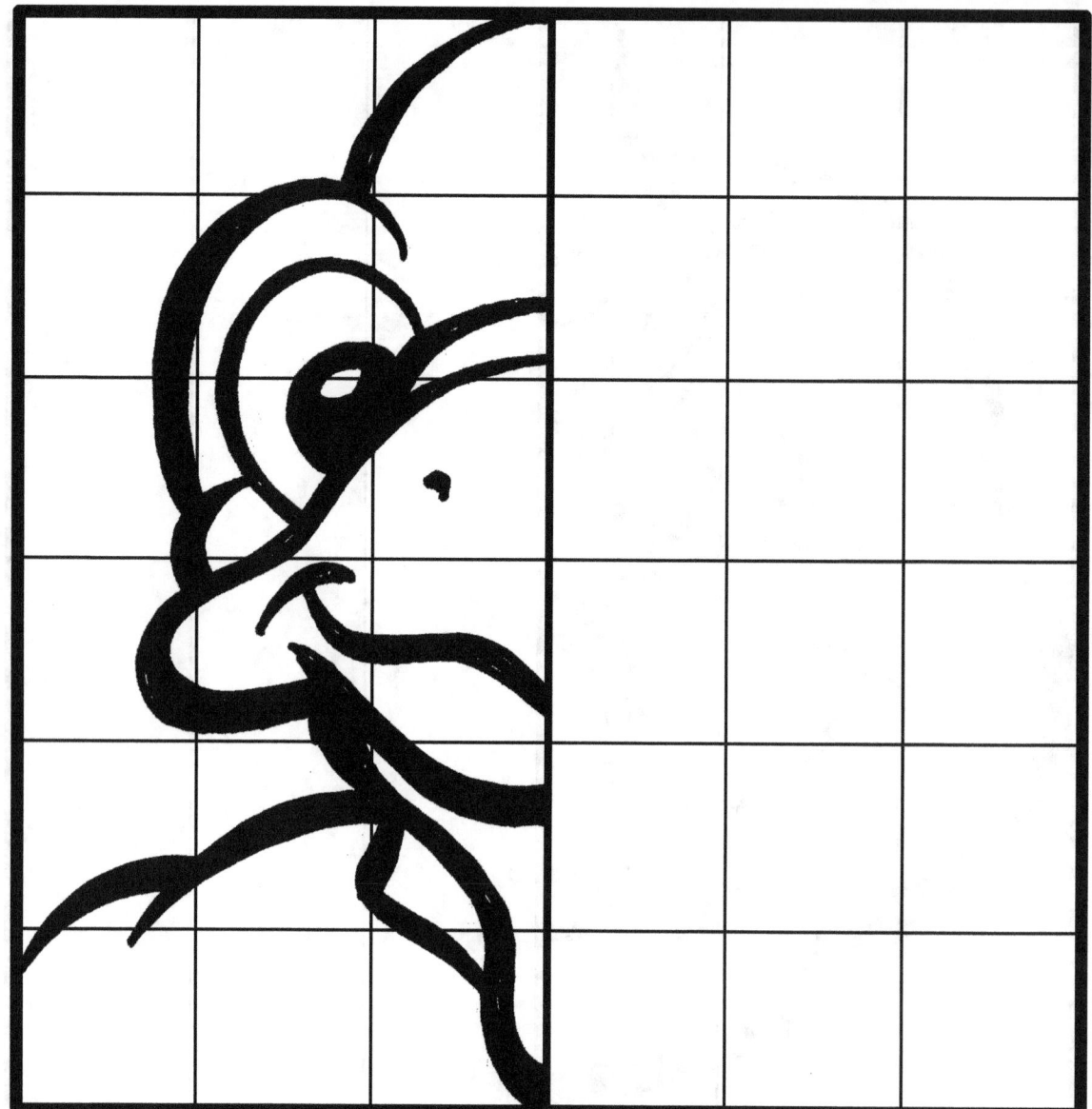

TURKEY

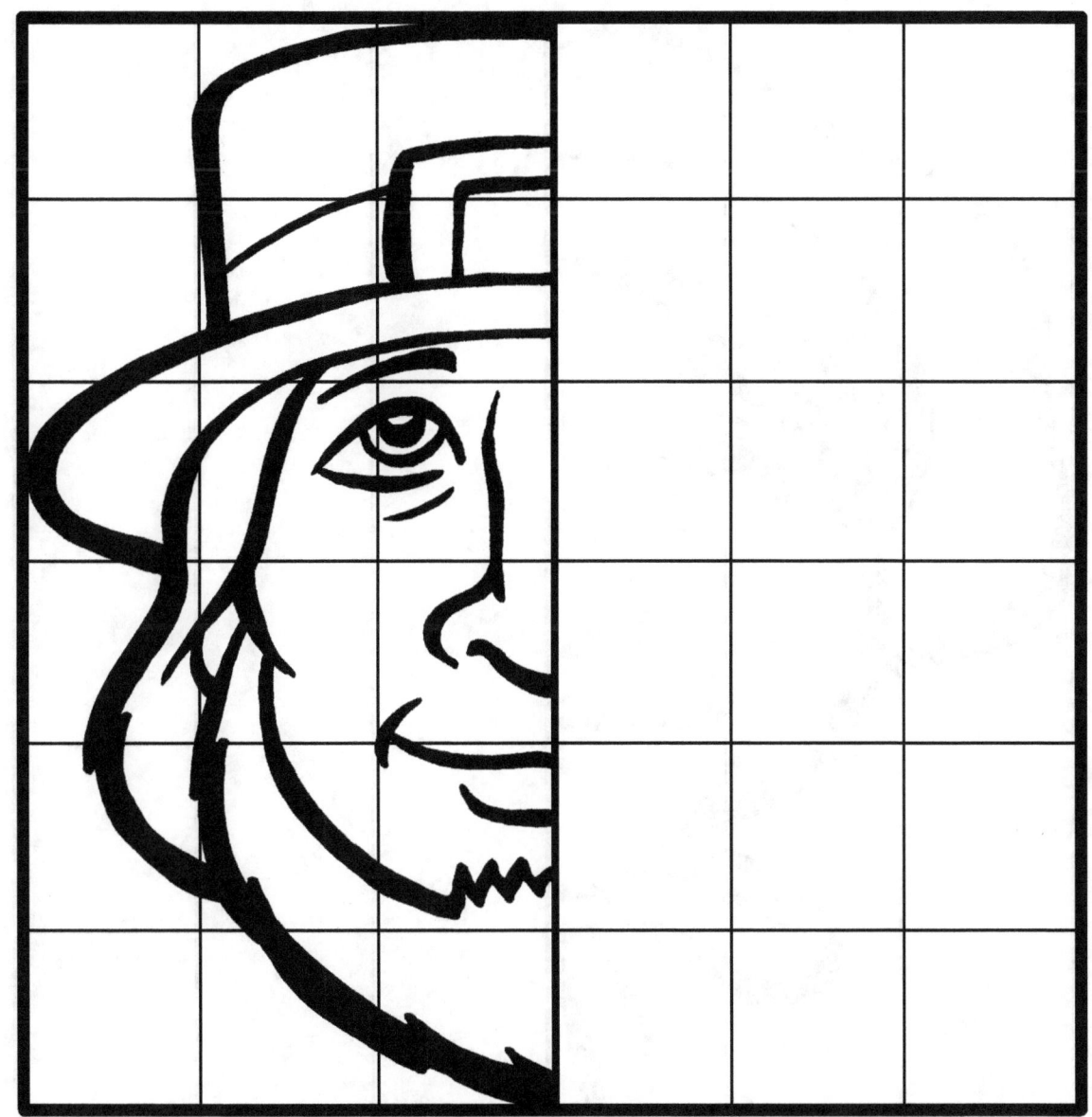

PILGRIM MAN

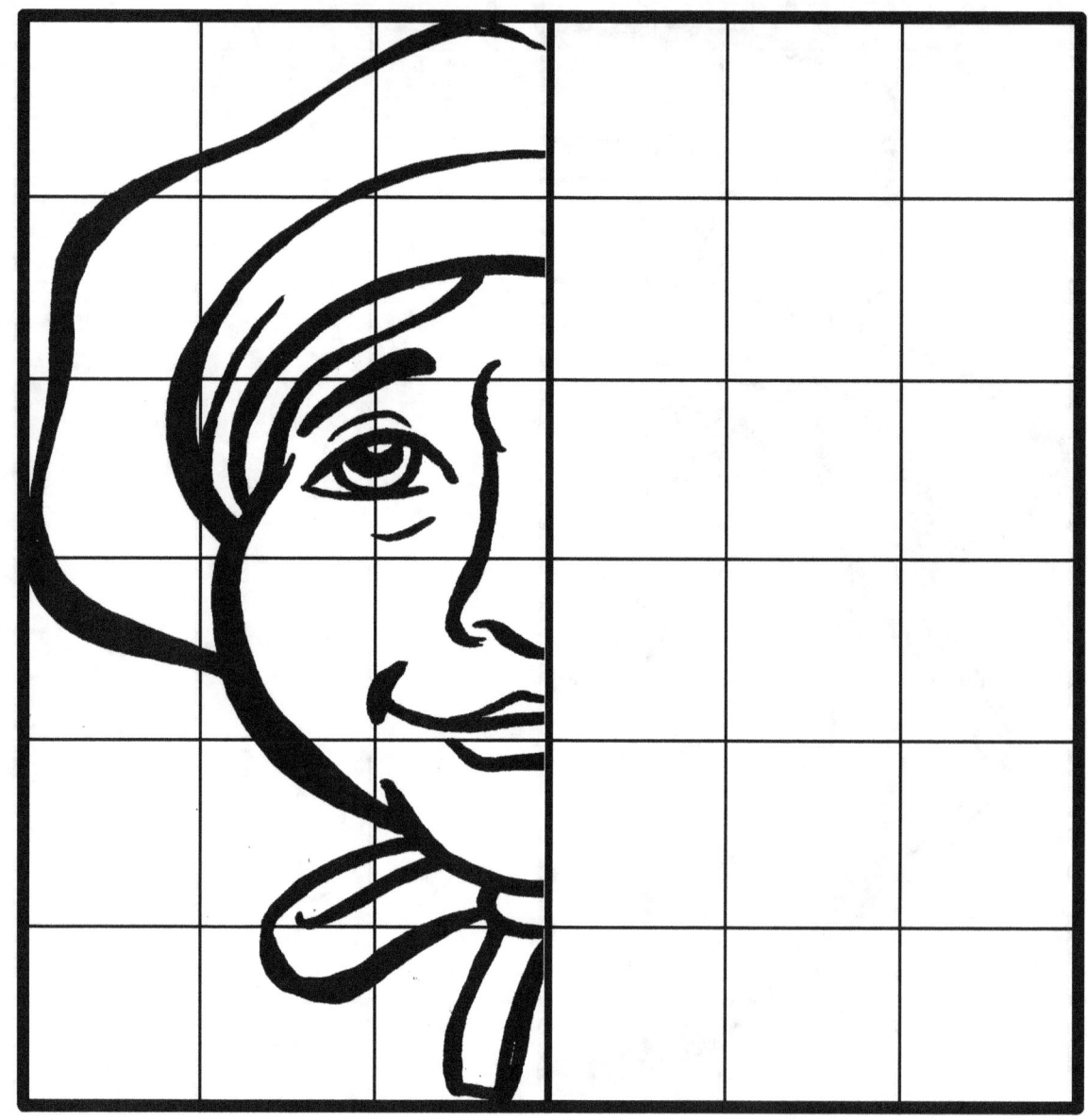

PILGRIM WOMAN

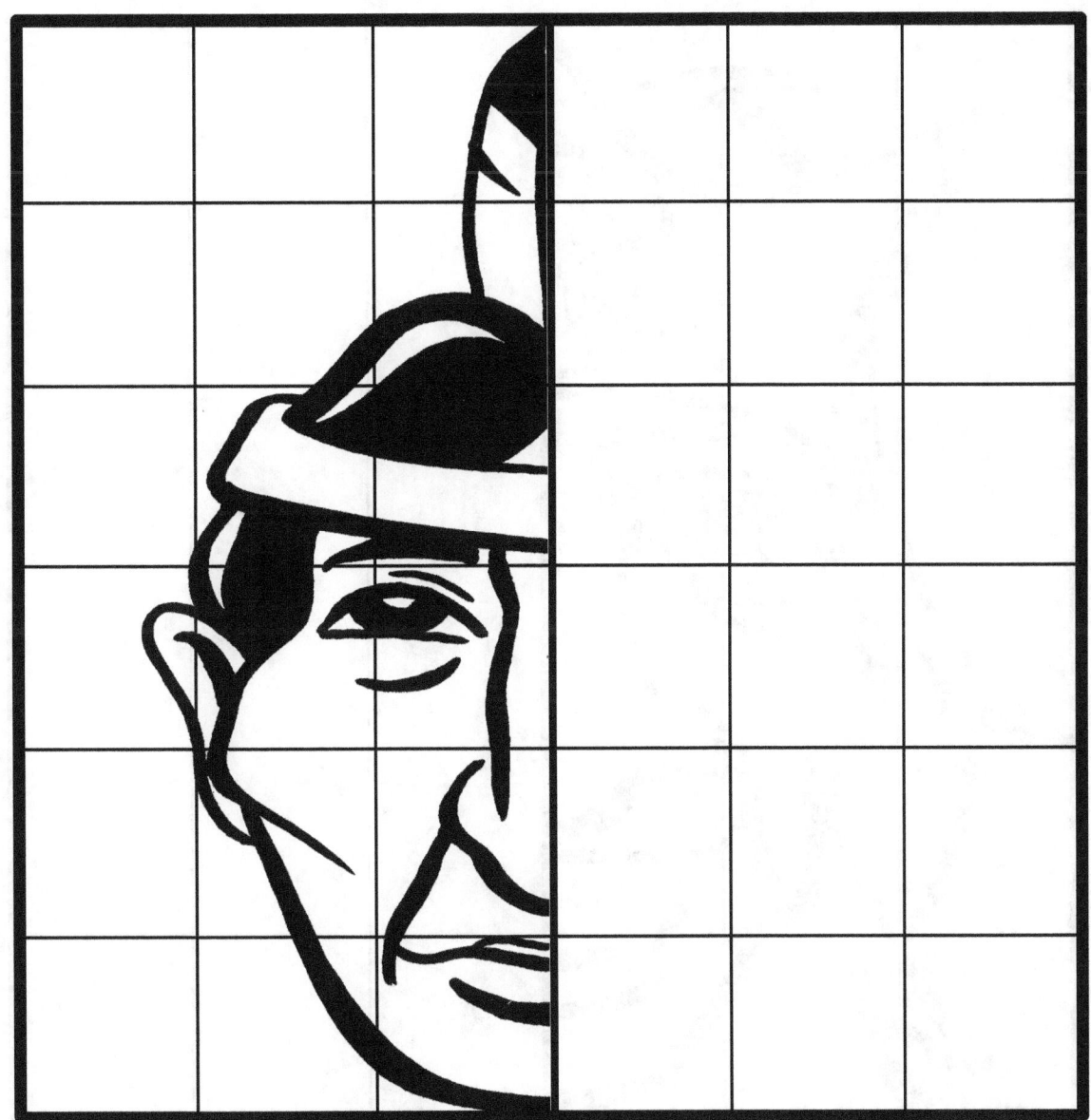

WAMPANOAG VISITOR

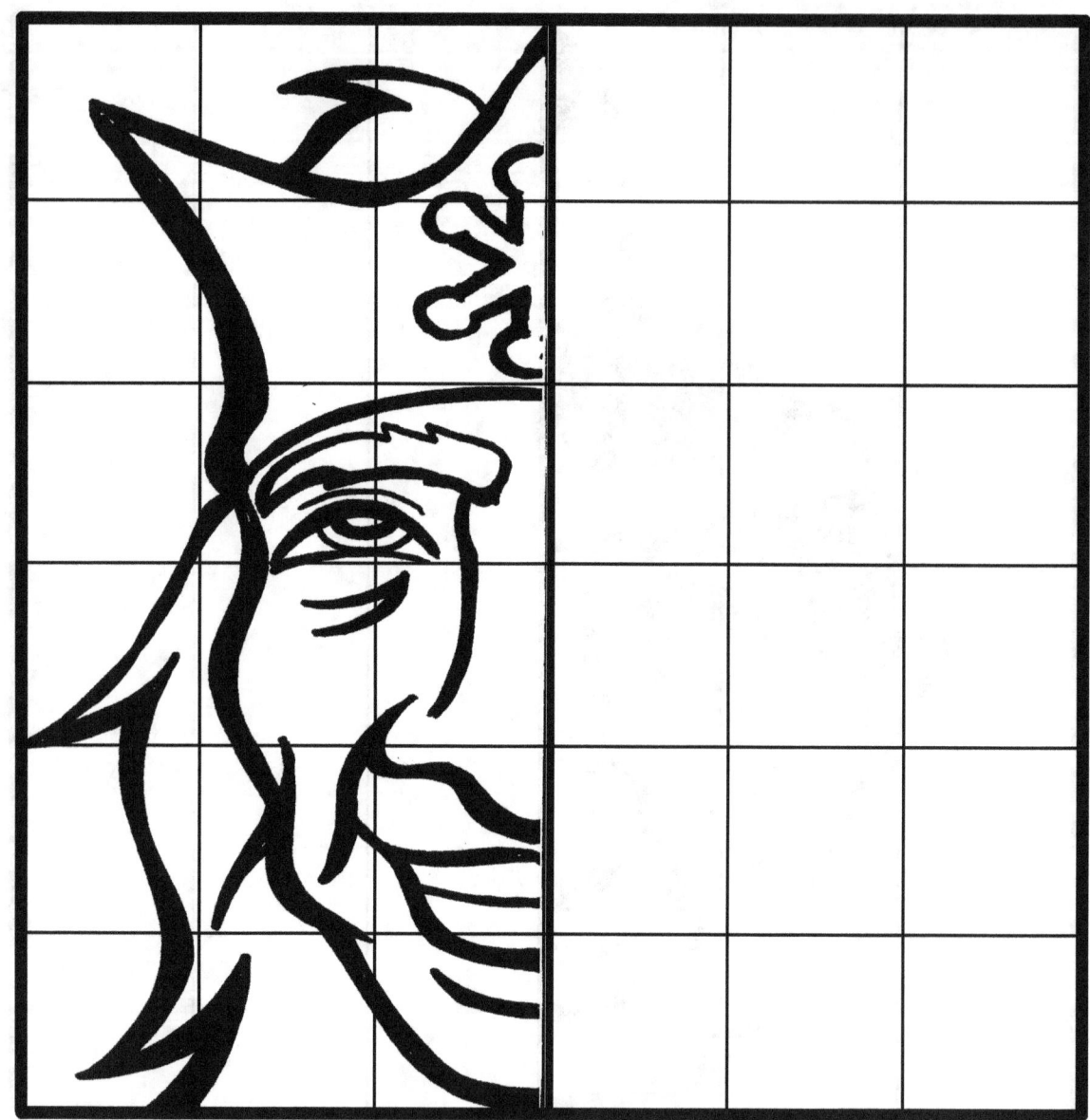

JACK FROST

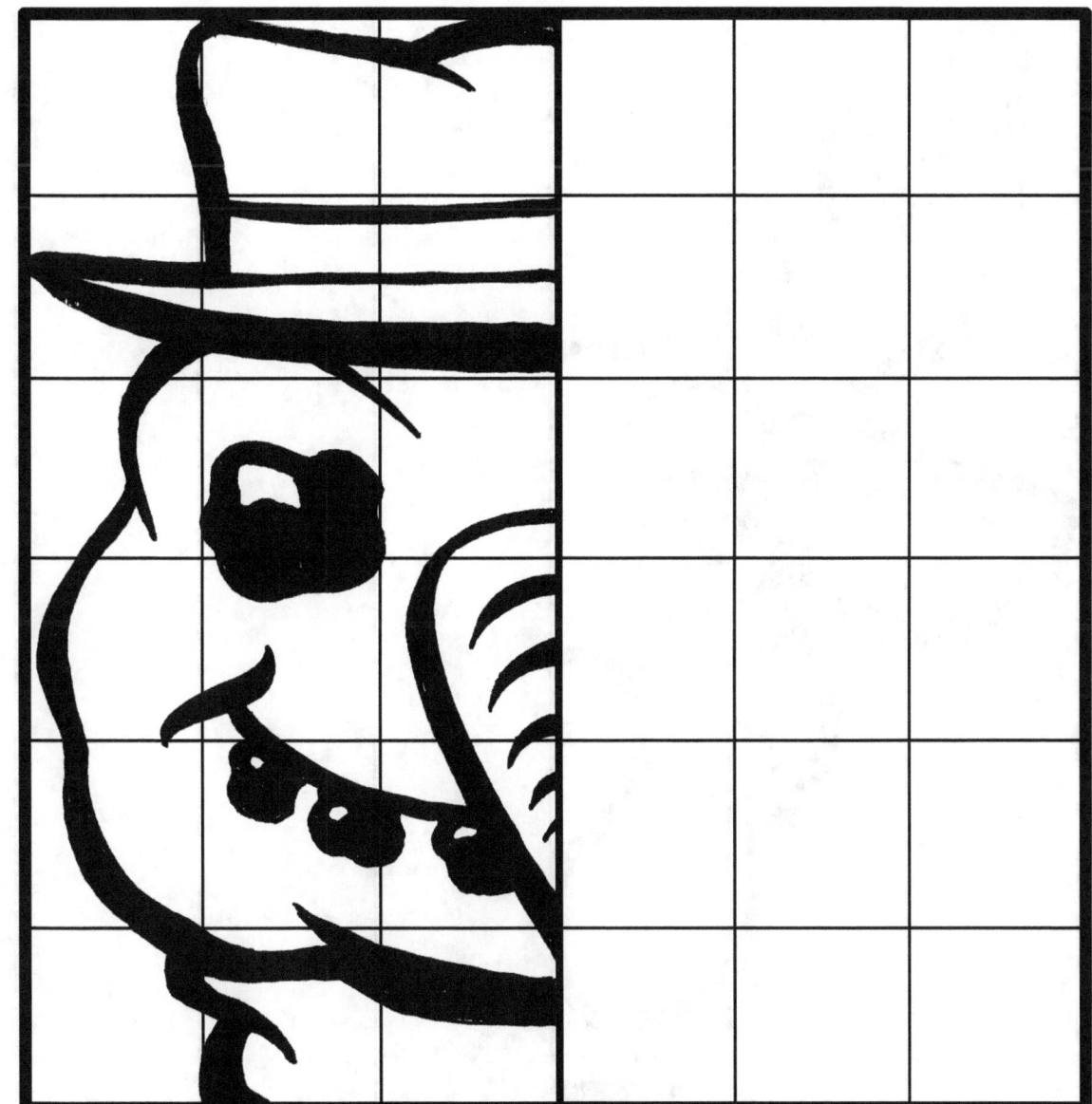

FROSHTY

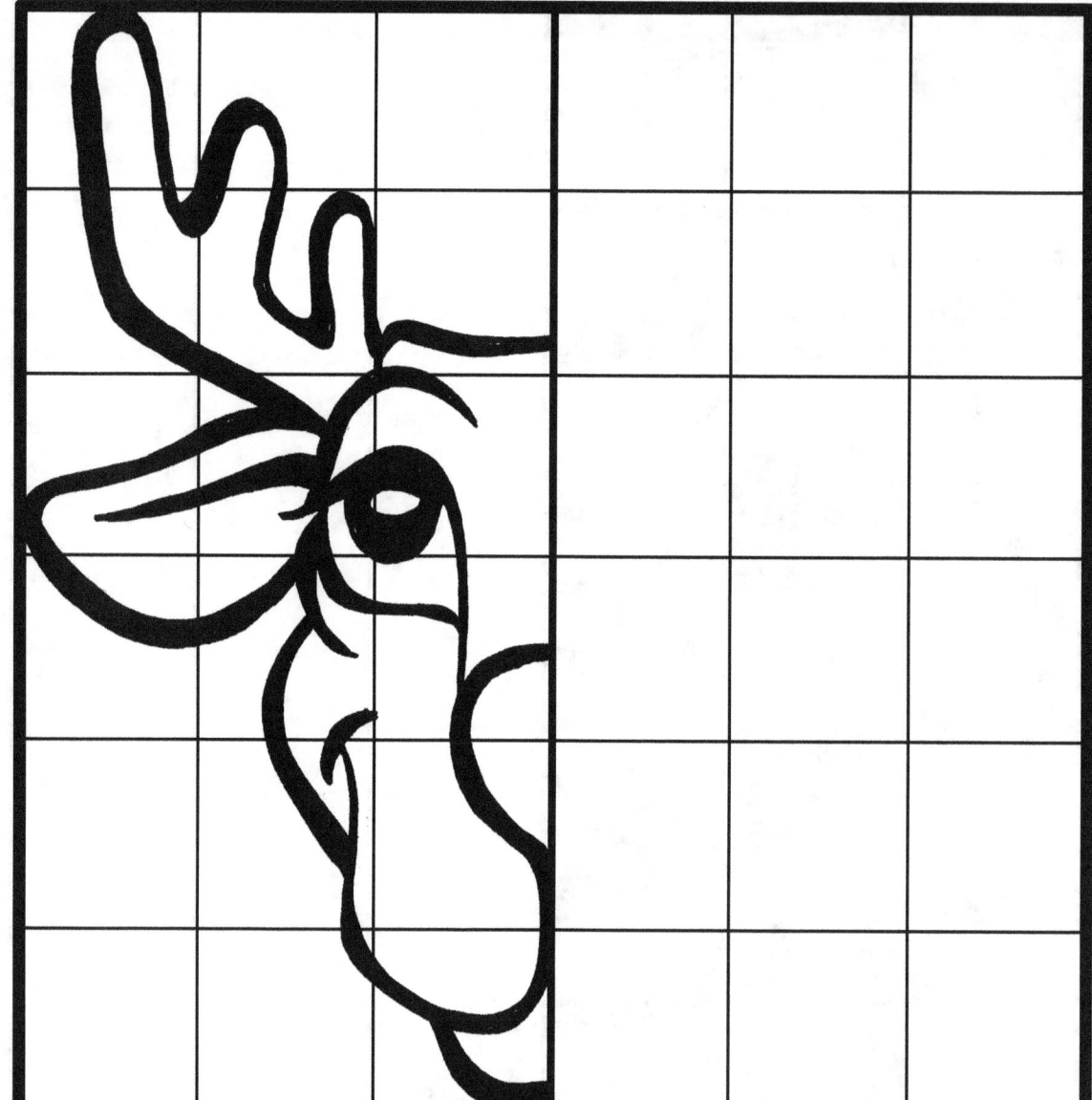

SPARKY

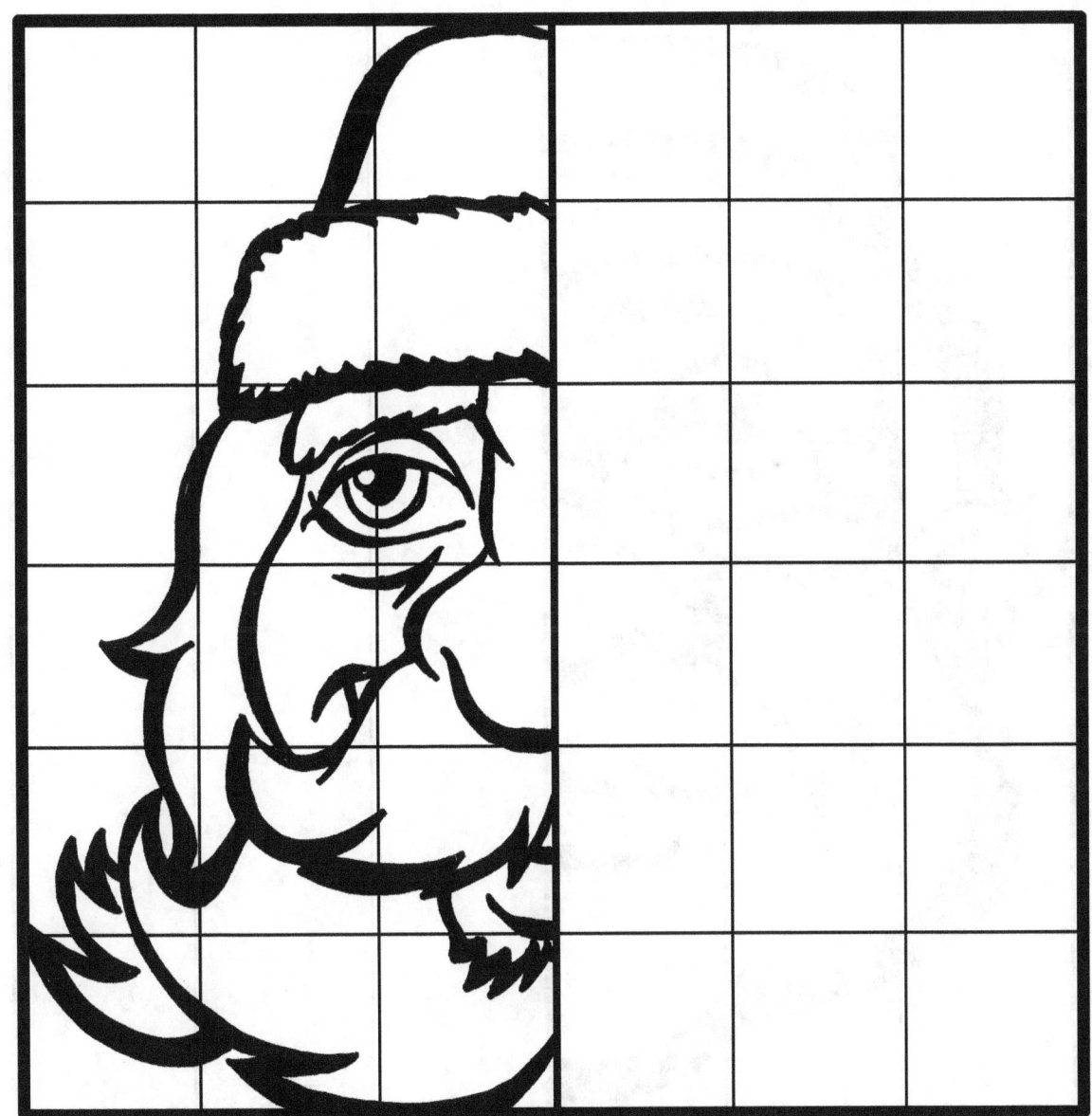

SANTA CLAUS

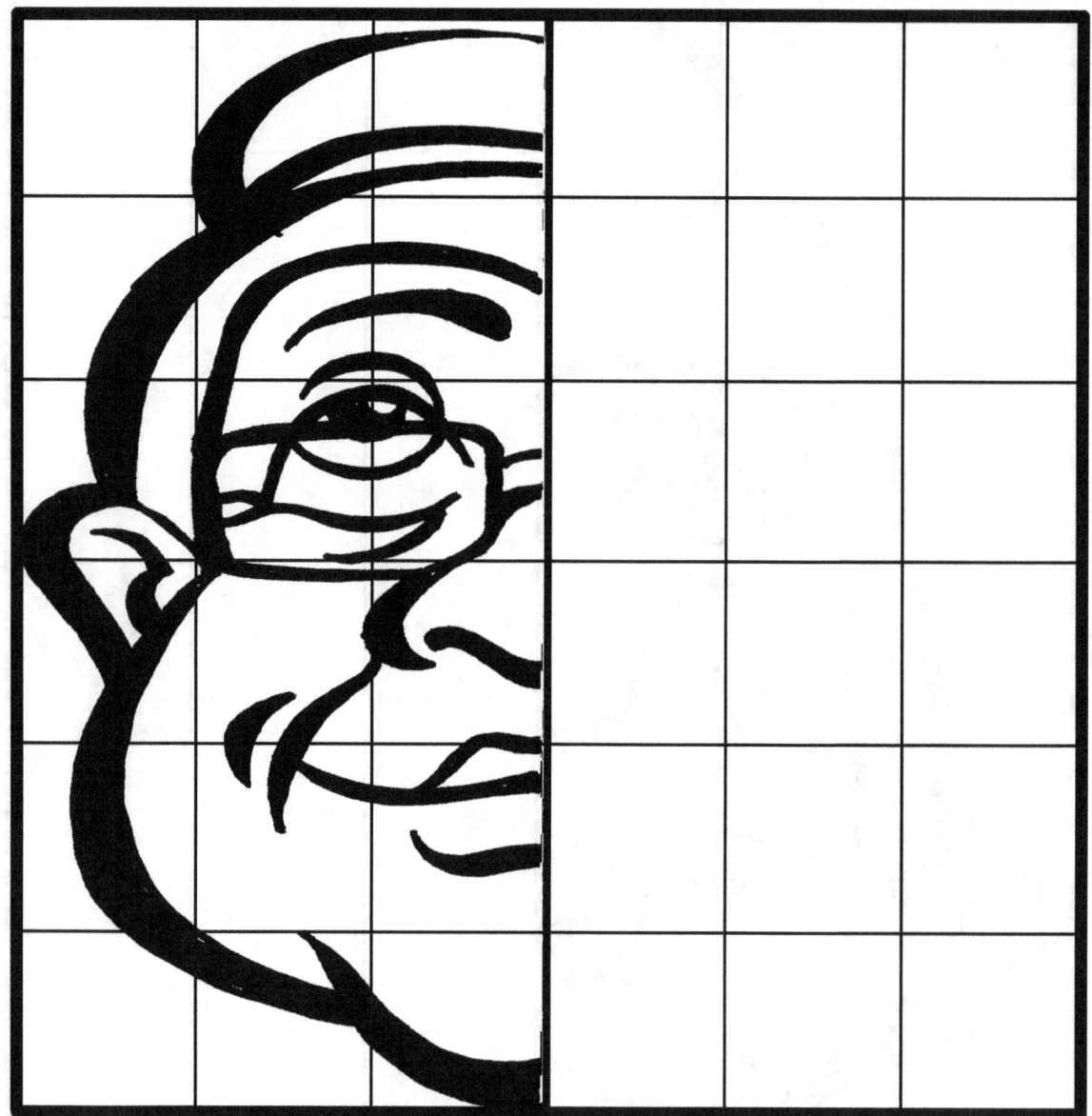

MRS. CLAUS

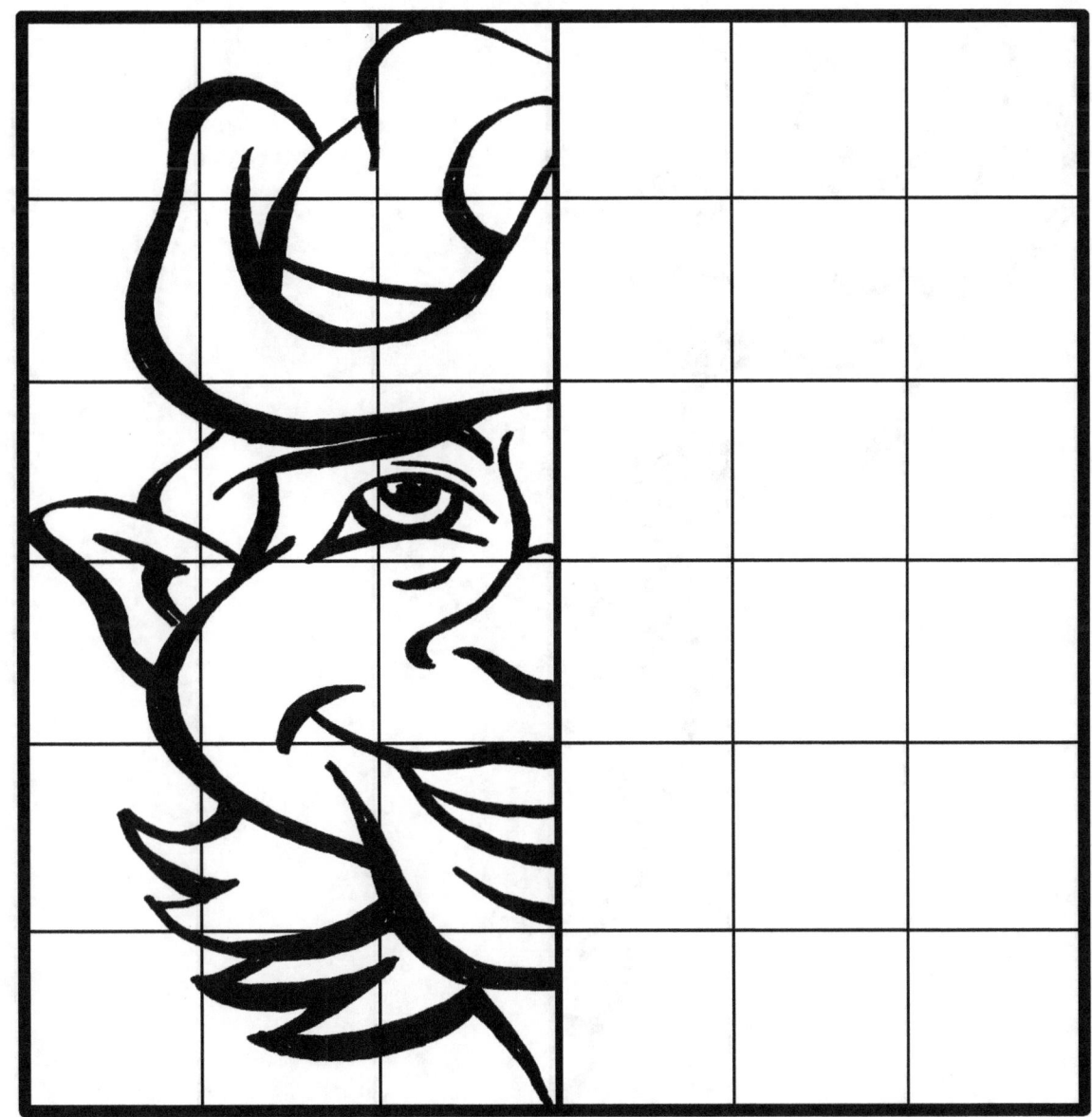

ELFY ELFENHEIMER

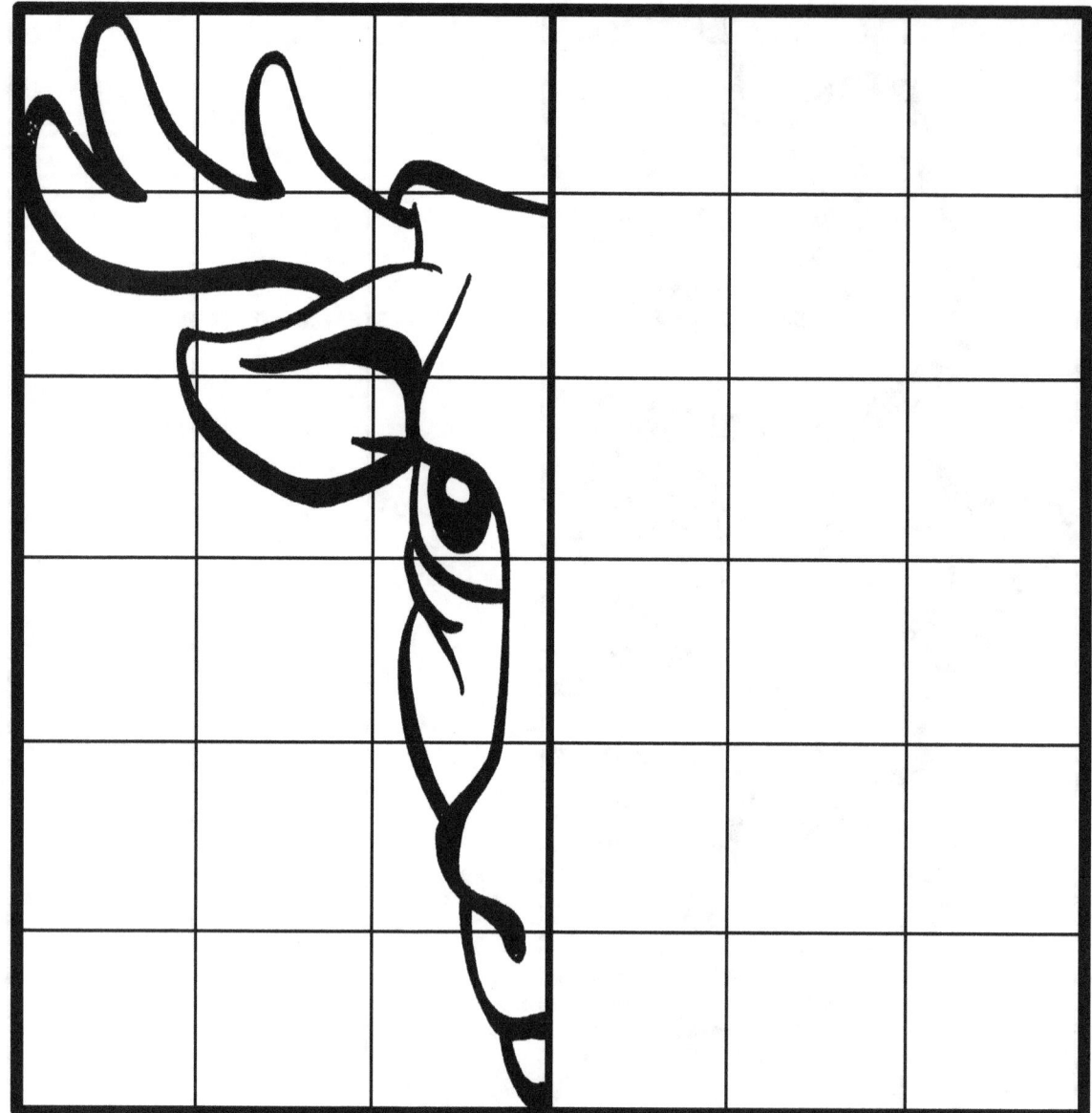

DANCER

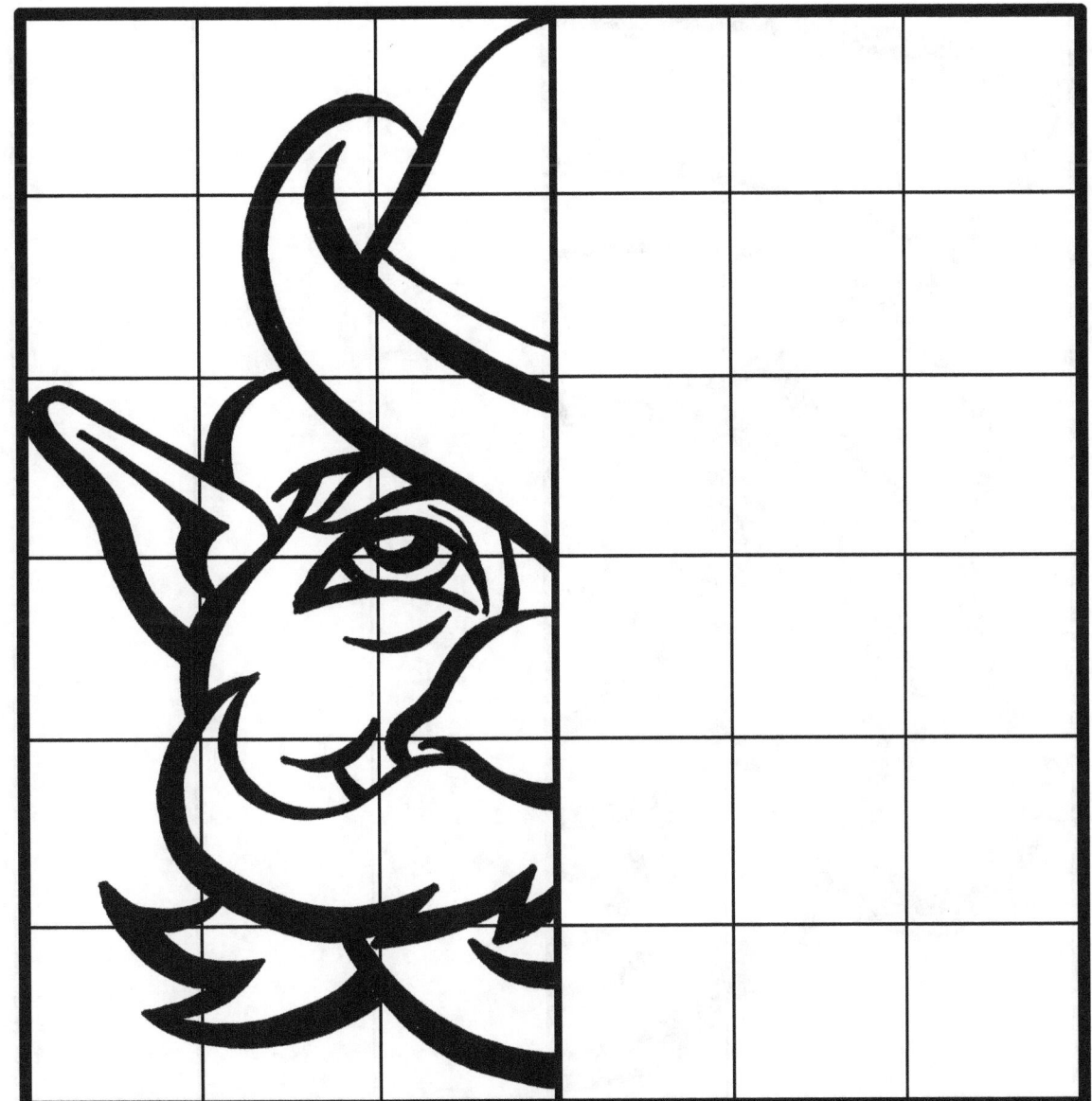

ELFENMEISTER

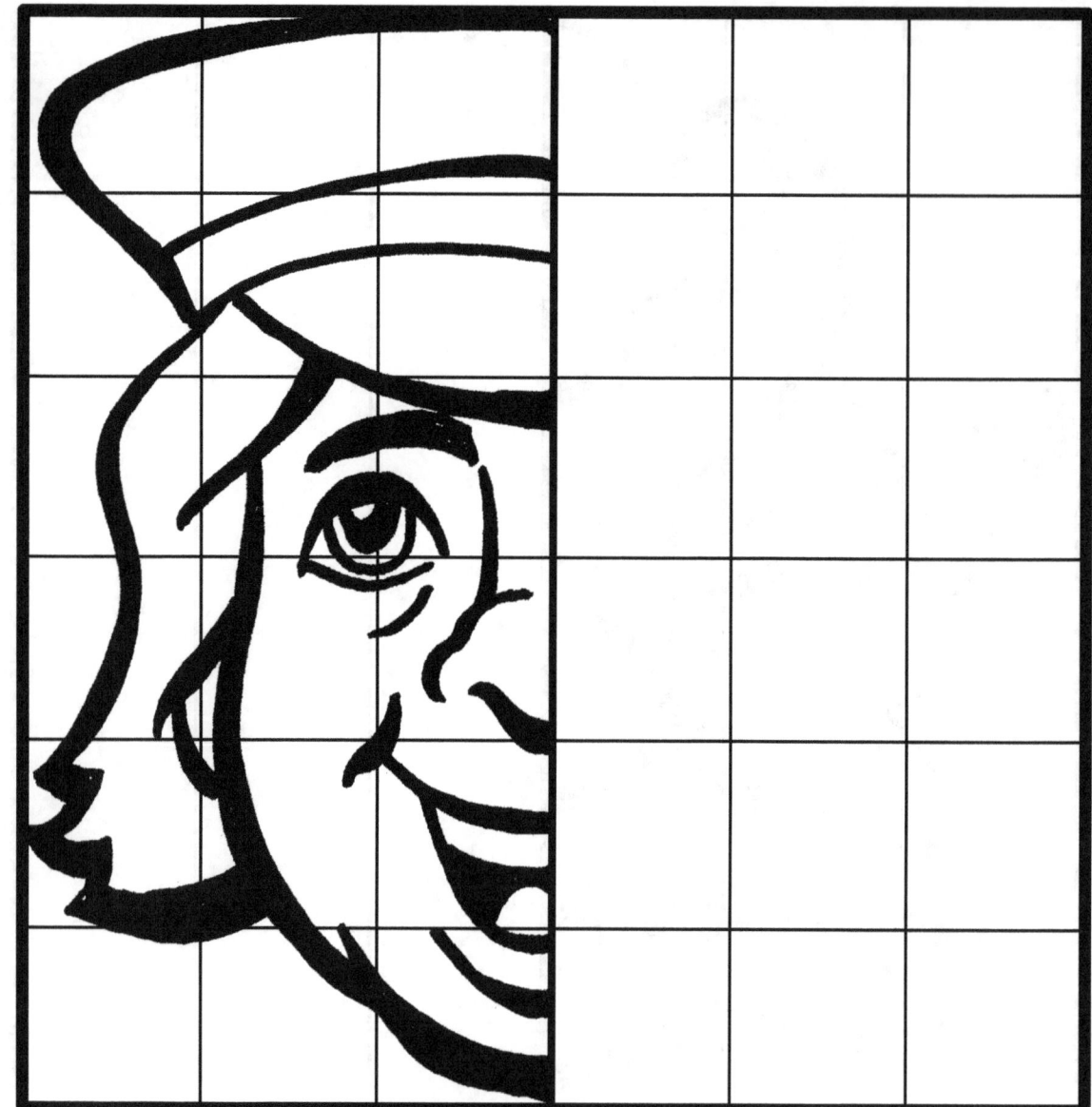

TINY TIM

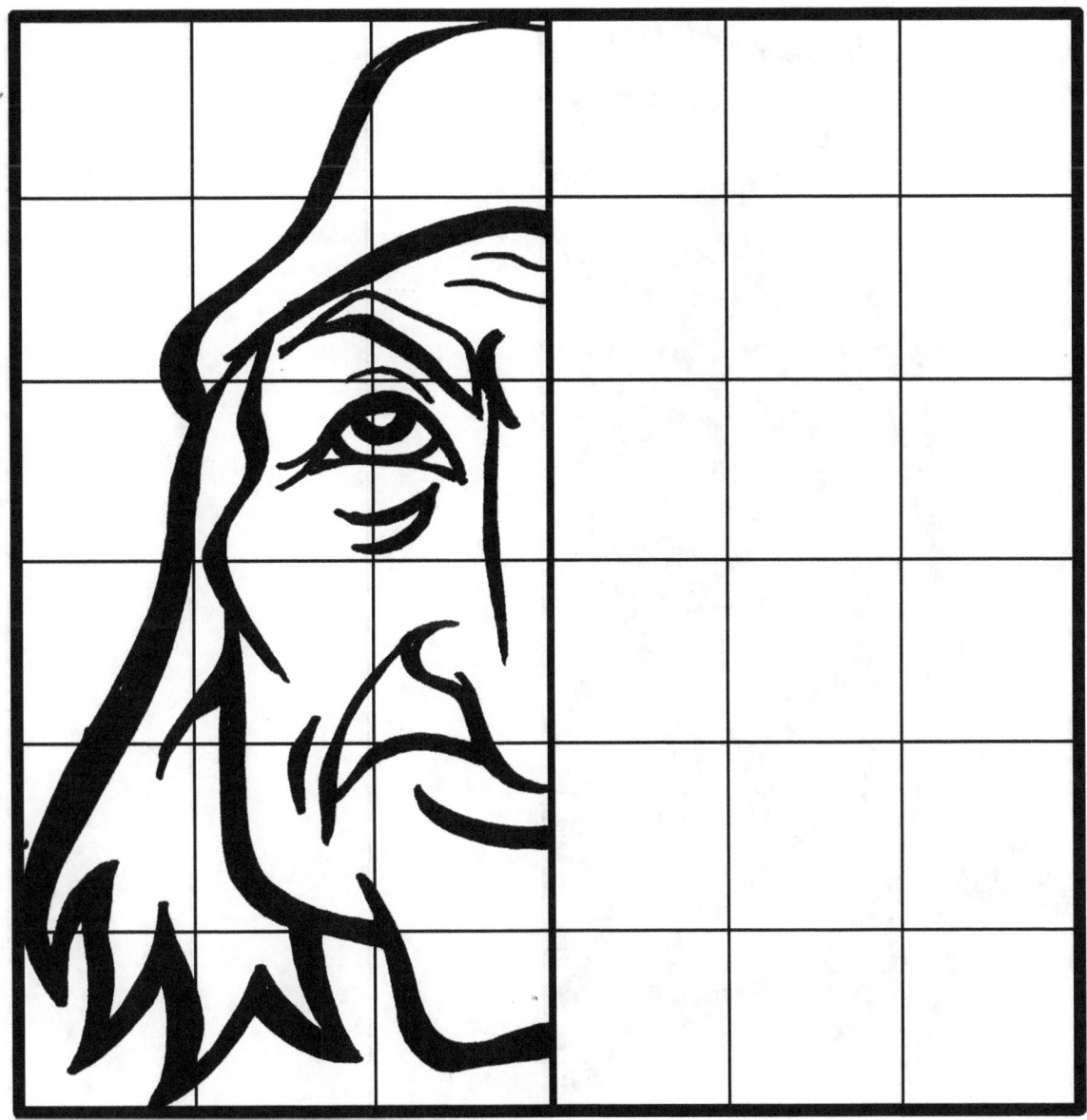

EBENEZER SCROOGE

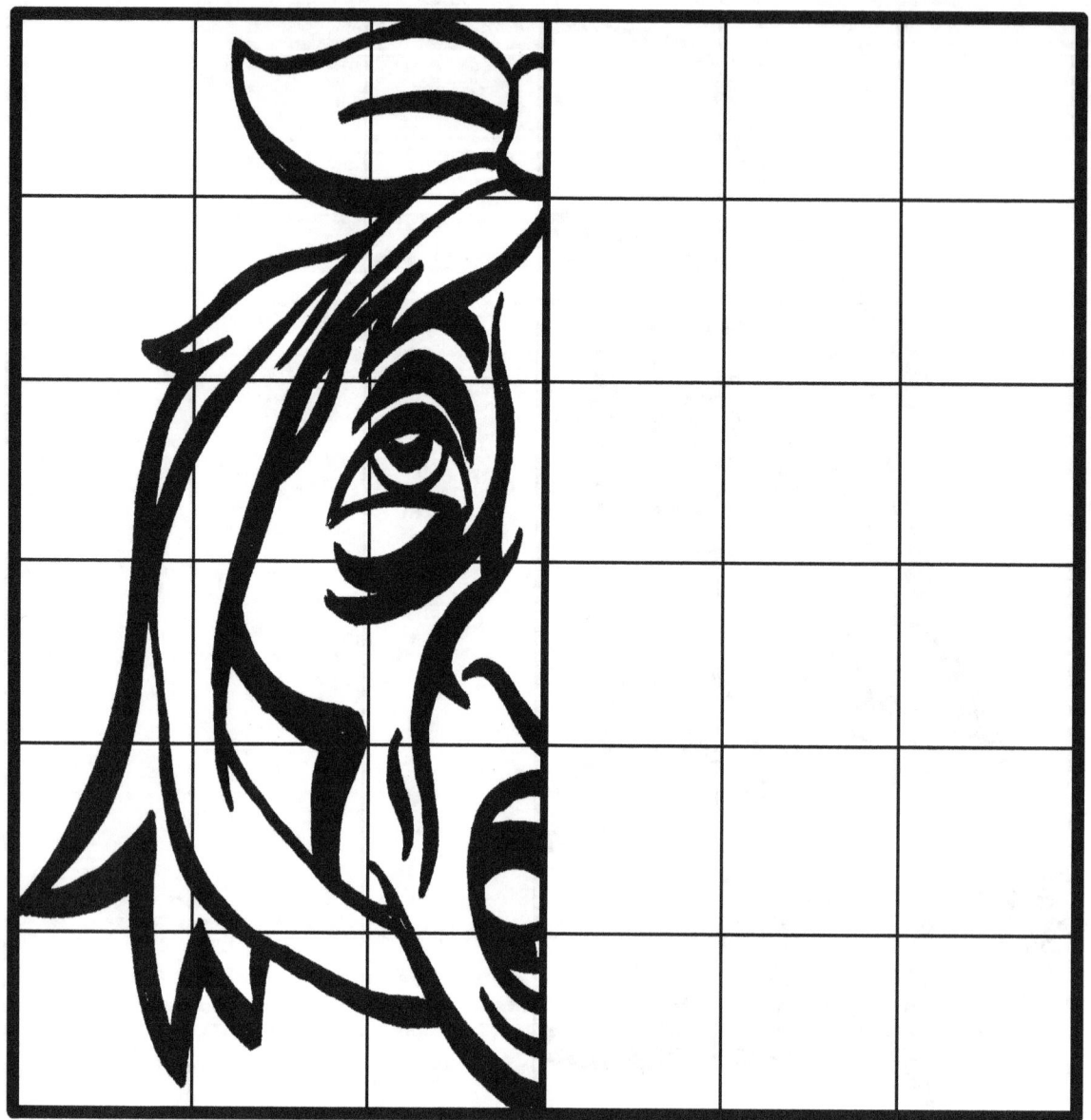

JACOB MARLEY

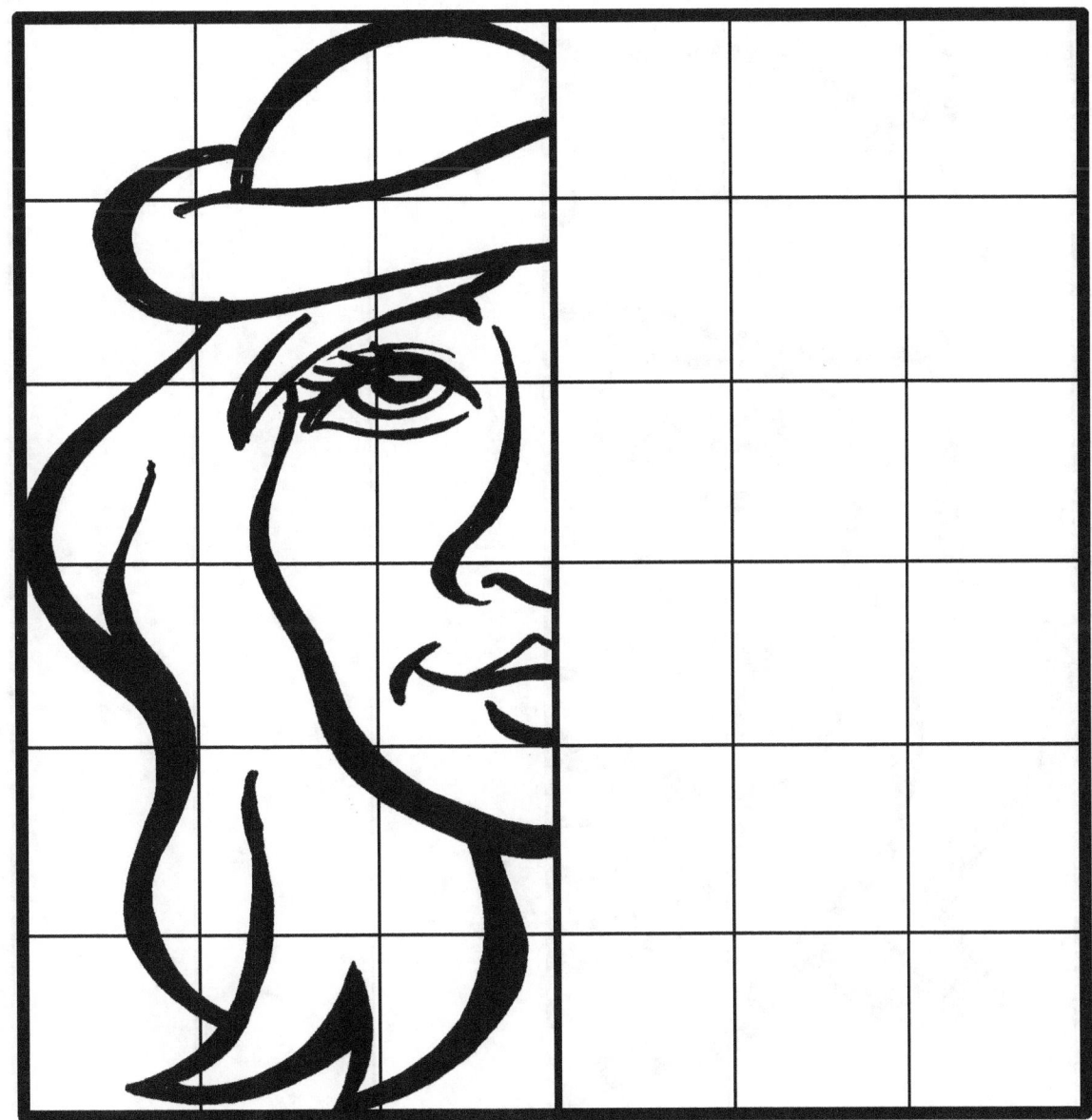

GHOST OF CHRISTMAS PAST

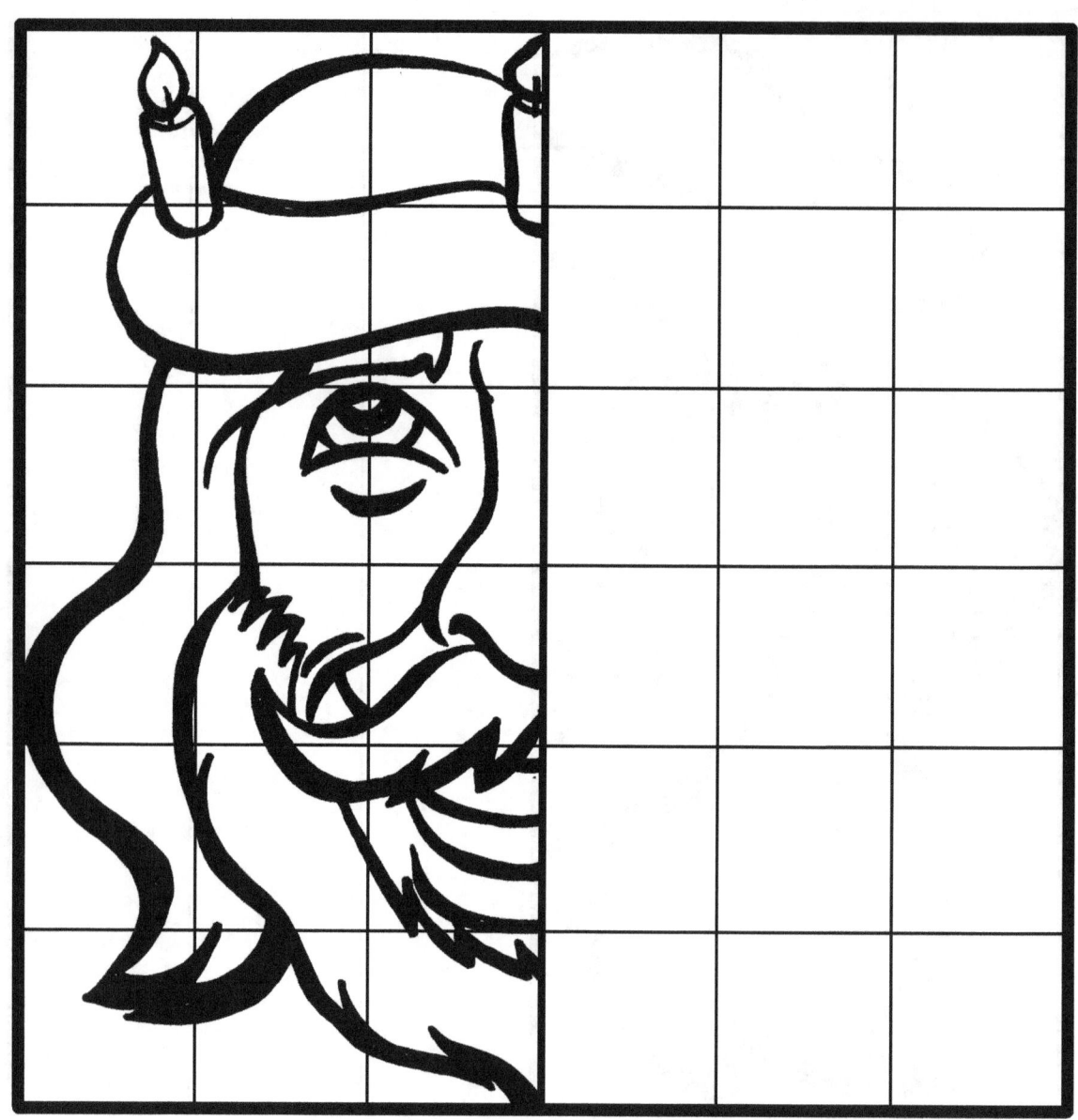

GHOST OF CHRISTMAS PRESENT

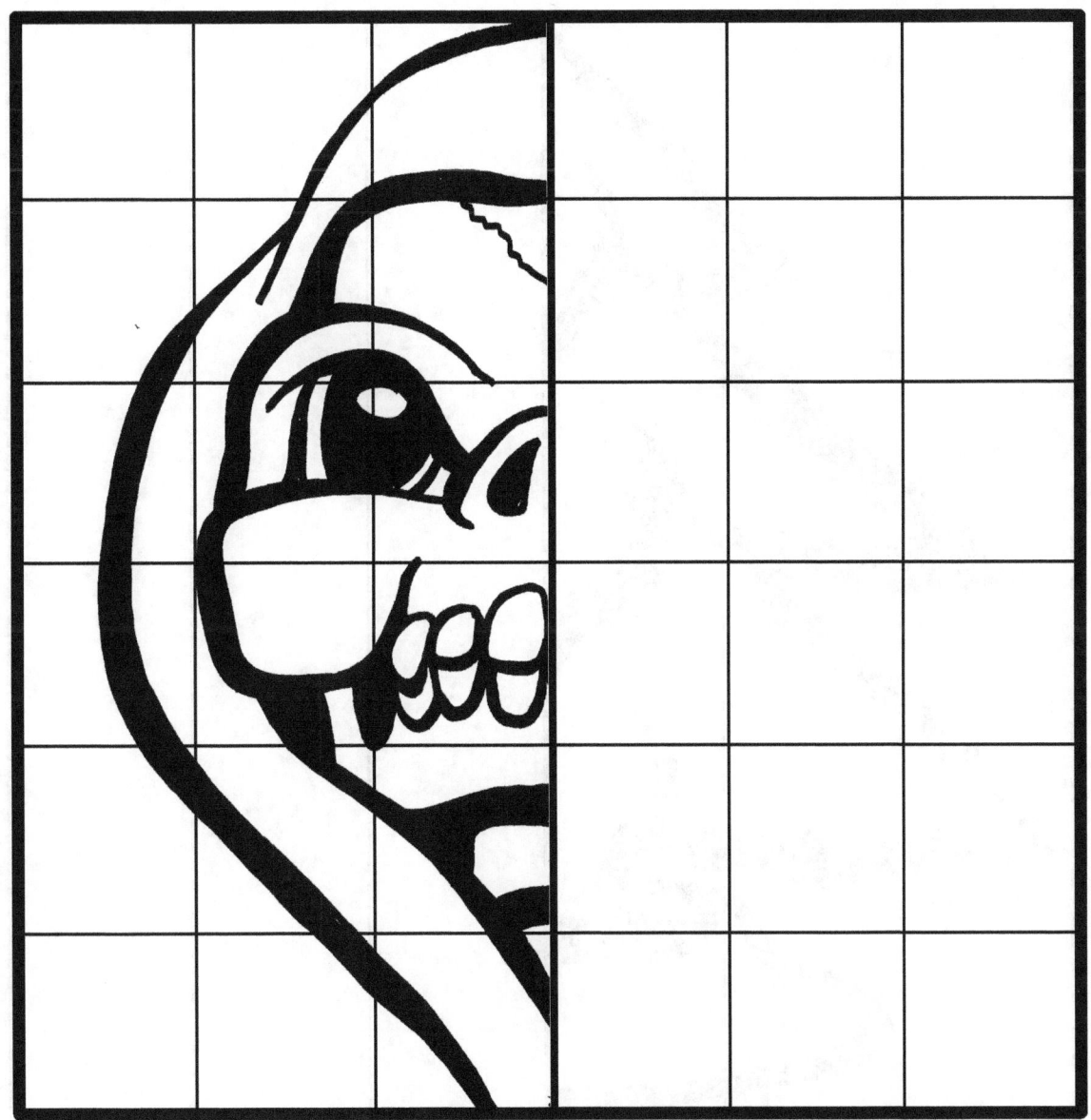

GHOST OF CHRISTMAS FUTURE

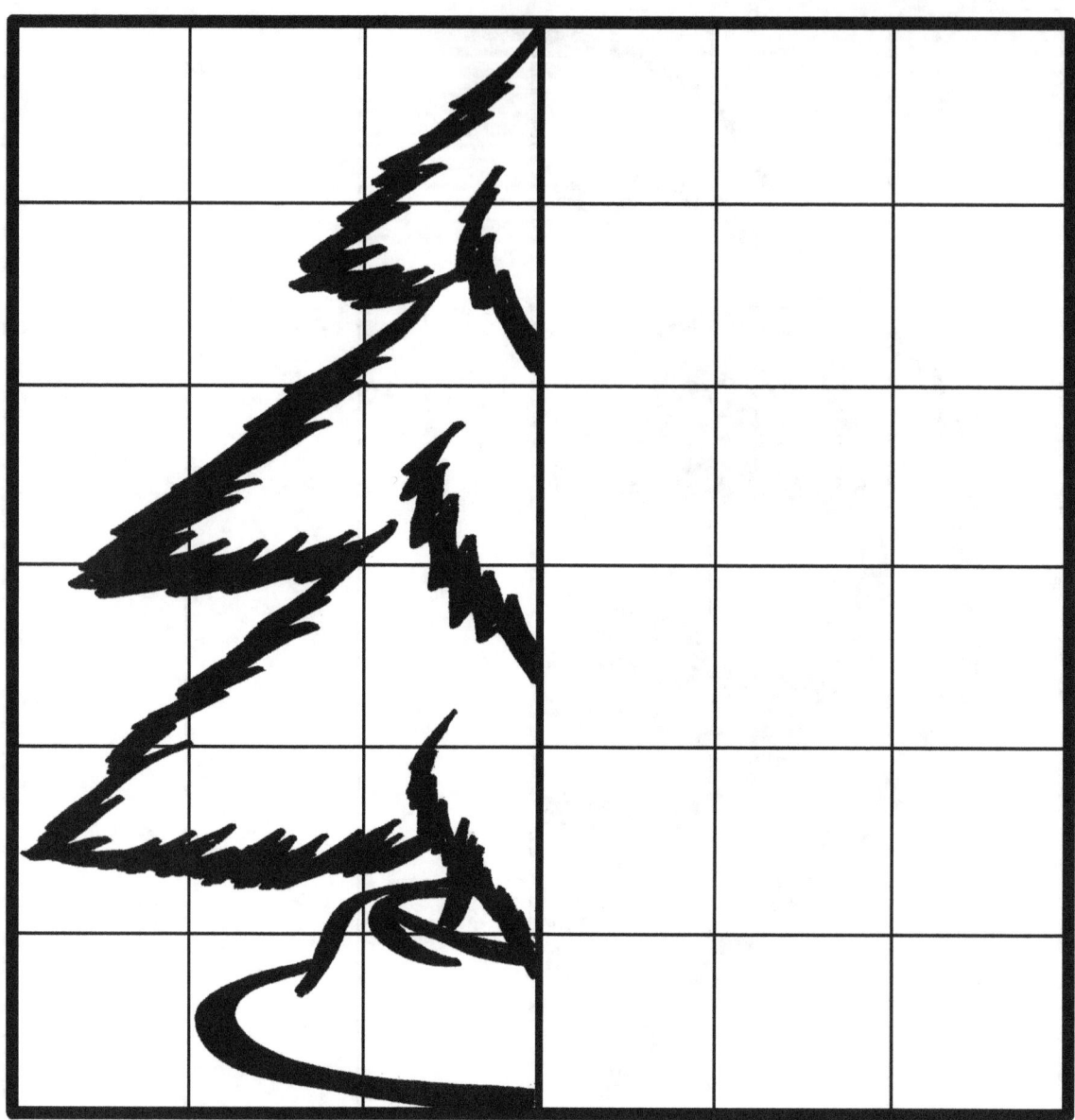

CHRISTMAS TREE
DRAW IT THEN DECORATE IT.

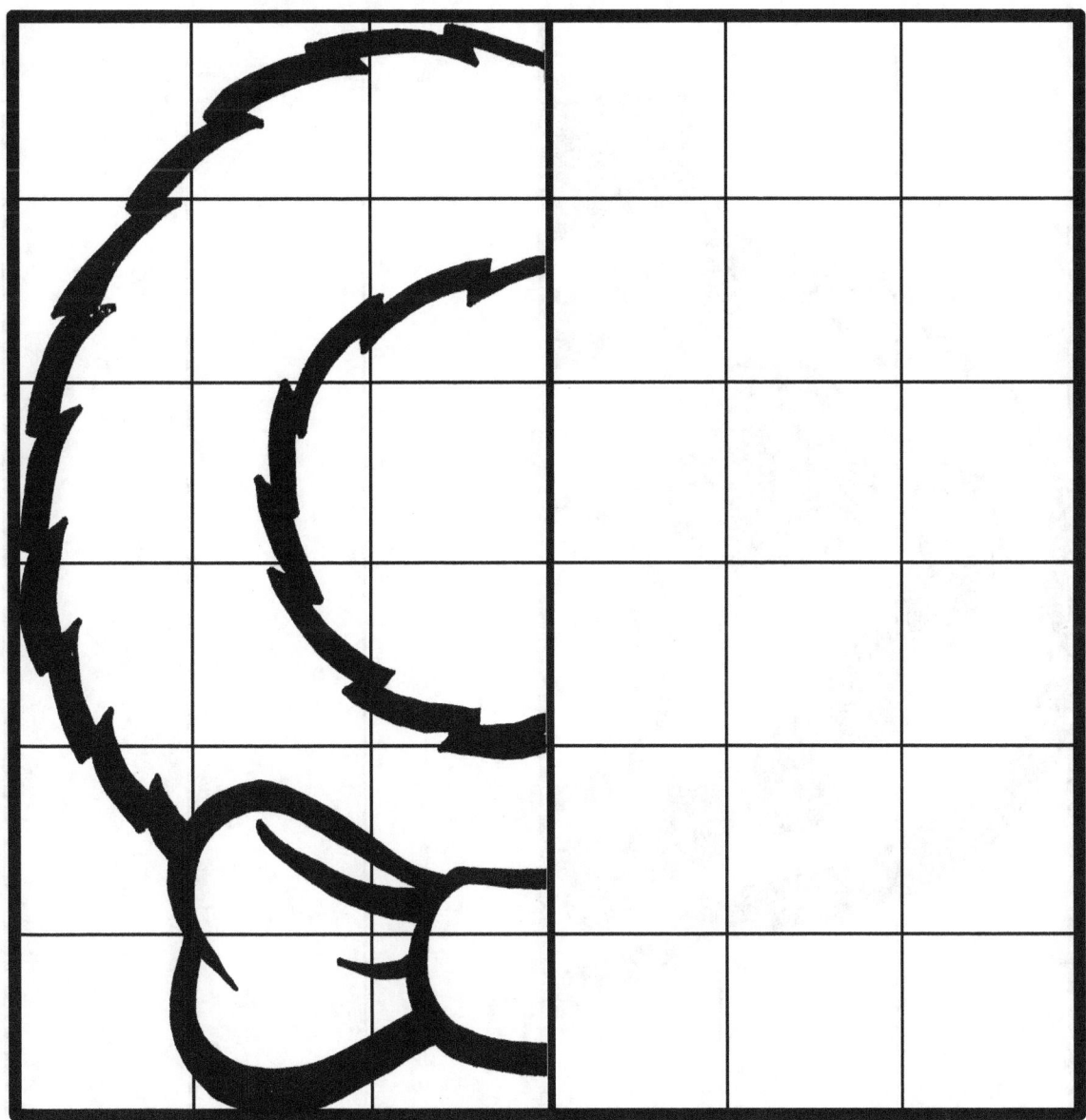

CHRISTMAS WREATH
DRAW IT THEN DECORATE IT.

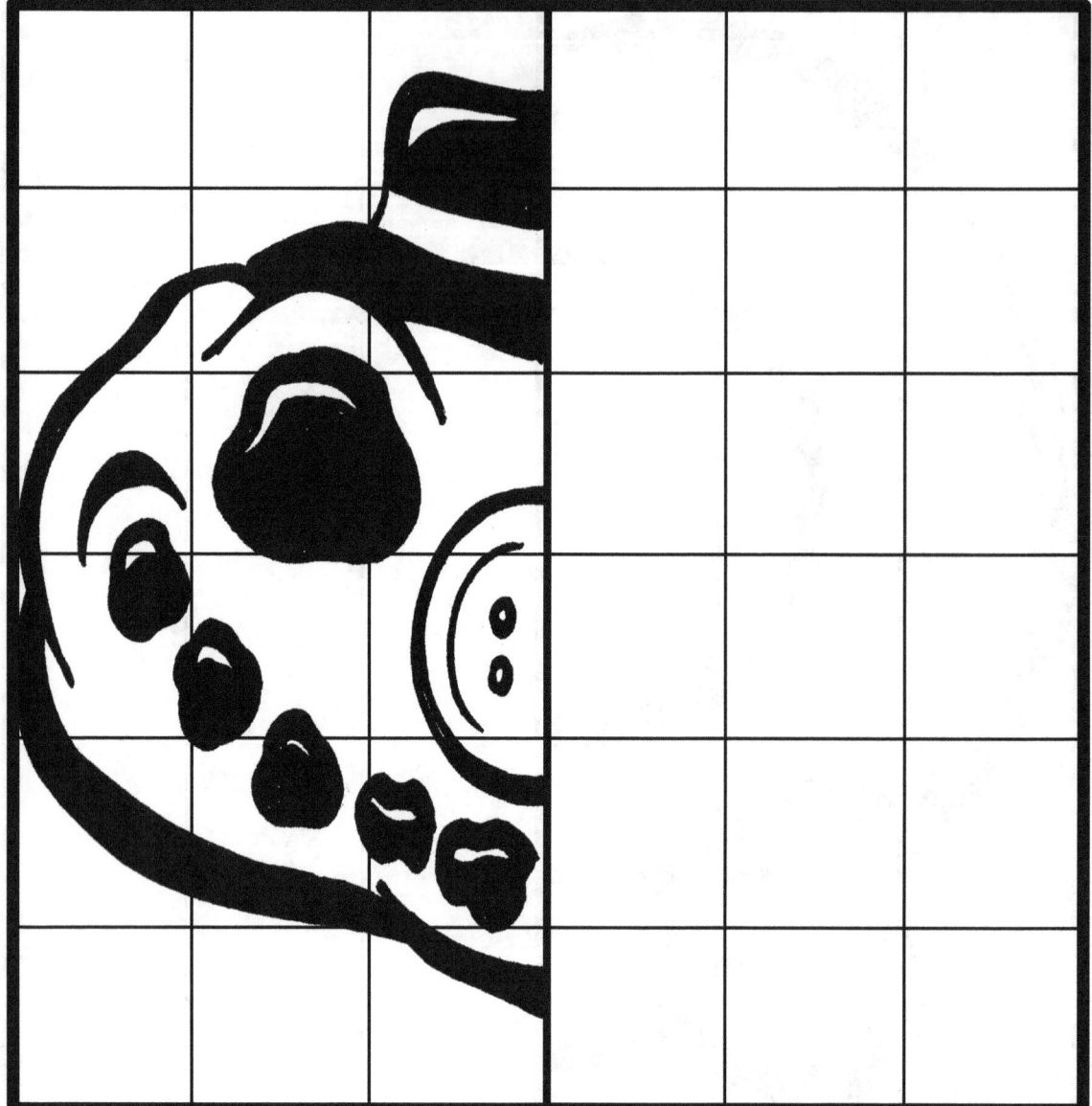

SLUSHY

Now that you have finished a a year's worth of holiday fun, finish me, Father Time, and then try a few of your own. On the next few pages are some blank grids. Draw half a face up to the middle line and then finish it just as you did all the others. Have fun!

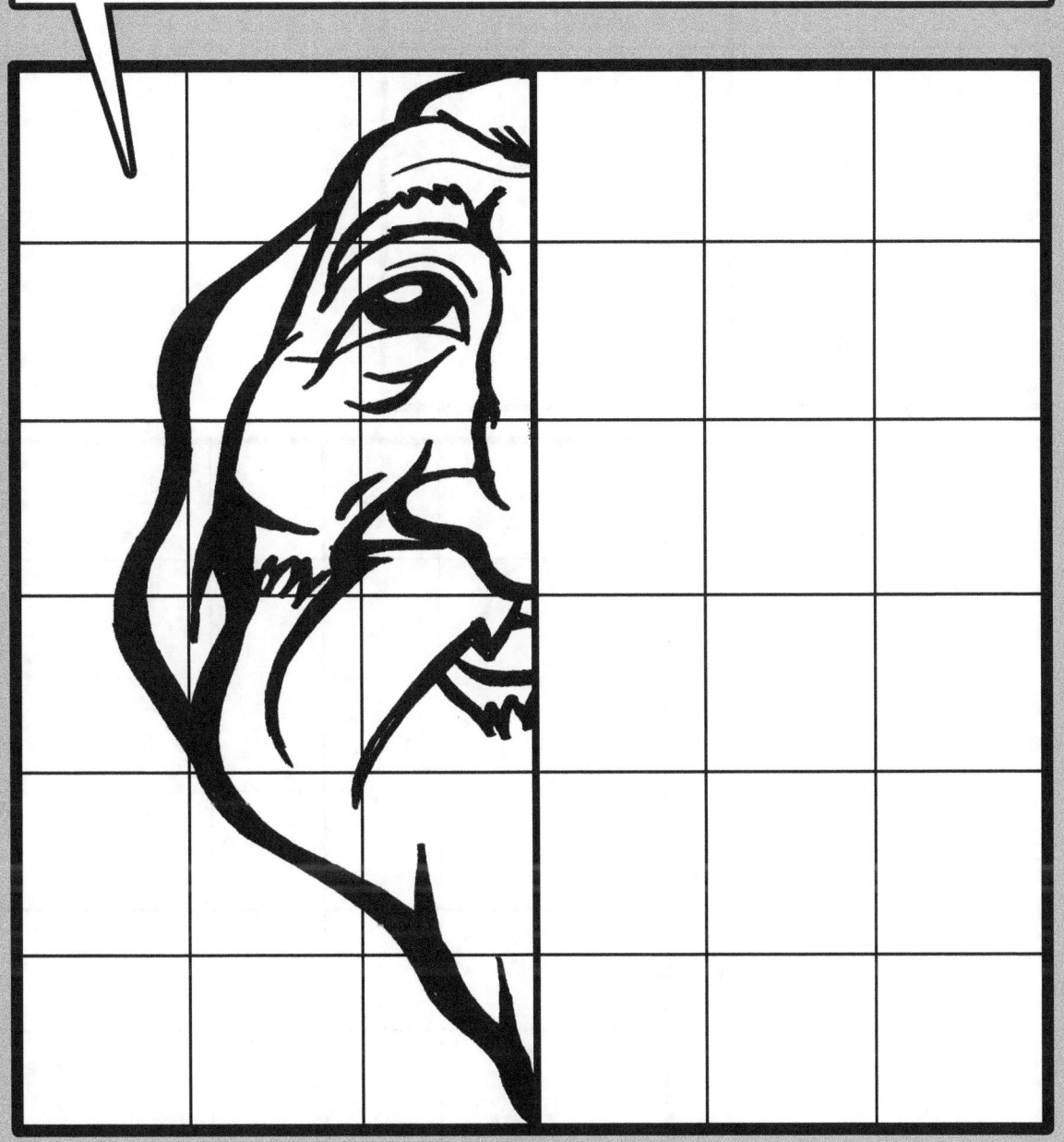

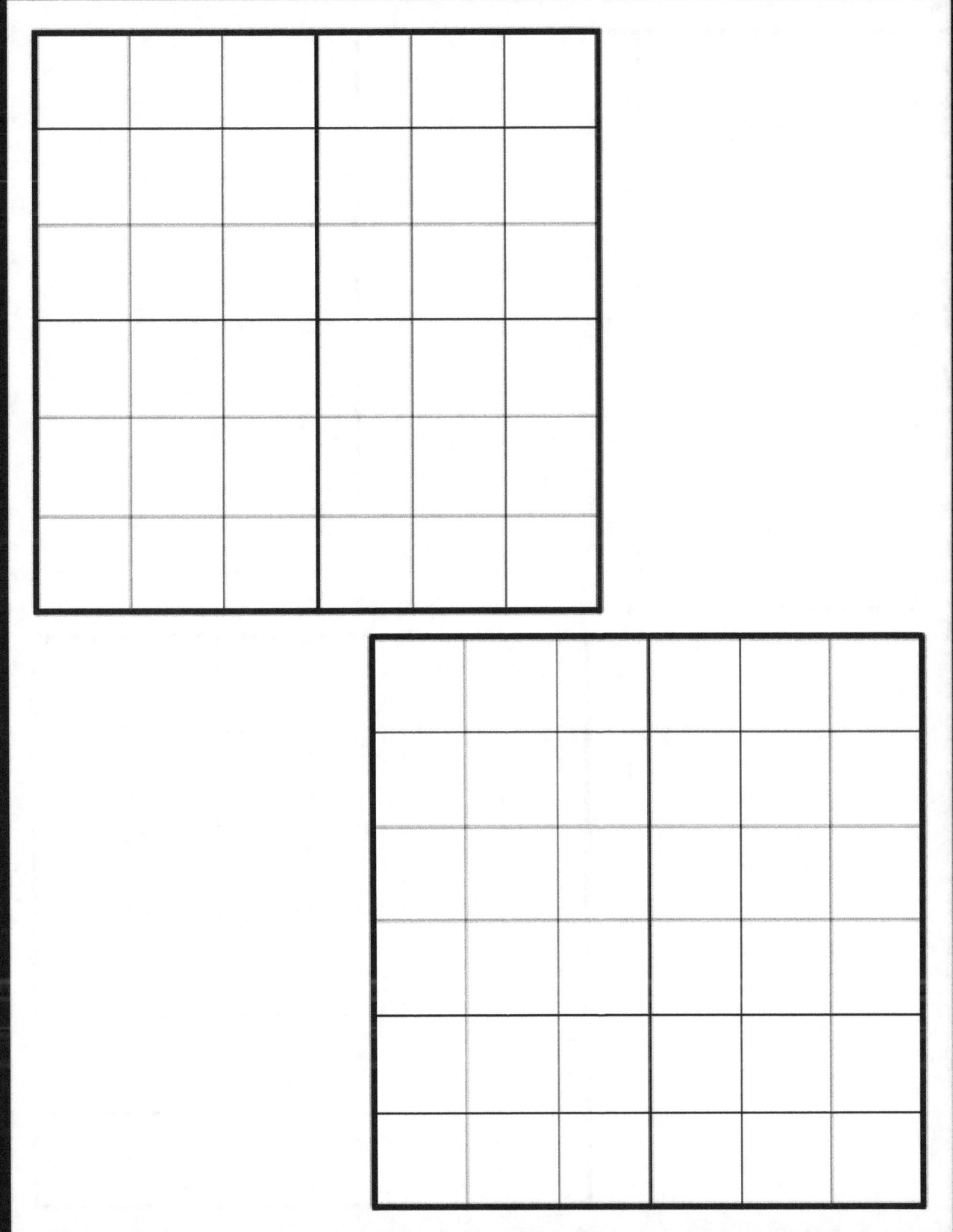

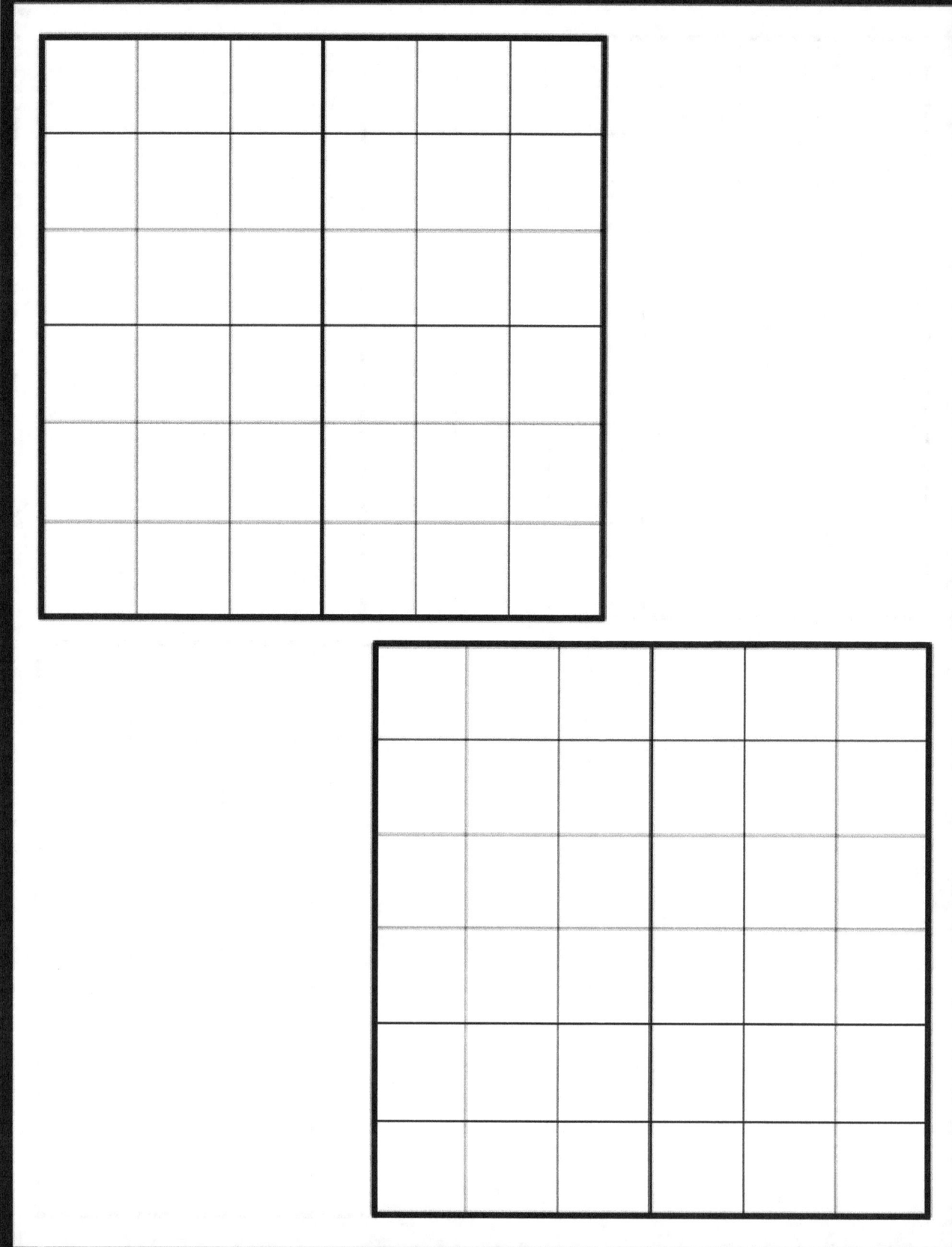

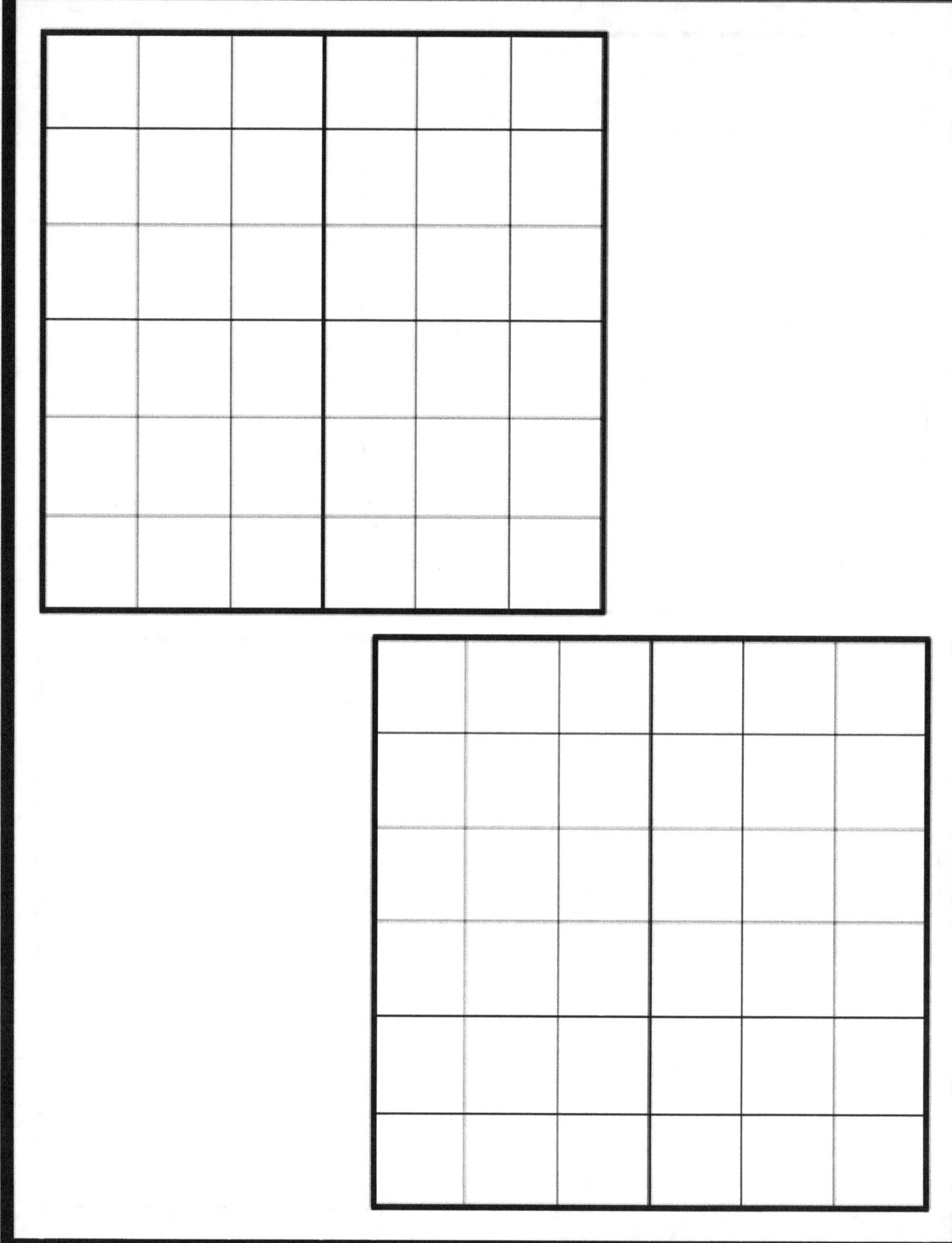

For more resources to build your creativity go to dweisscreative.com

www.ingramcontent.com/pod-product-compliance
Lightning Source LLC
Chambersburg PA
CBHW080606180526
45168CB00007B/2797